C000070489

BEING FAITHFUL

THE SHAPE OF HISTORIC ANGLICANISM TODAY

A COMMENTARY ON THE JERUSALEM DECLARATION

SUPPLEMENTED BY

THE WAY, THE TRUTH AND THE LIFE –

THEOLOGICAL RESOURCES FOR A PILGRIMAGE TO A GLOBAL ANGLICAN FUTURE

PREPARED BY THE THEOLOGICAL RESOURCE GROUP OF THE GLOBAL ANGLICAN FUTURE CONFERENCE (GAFCON)

GENERAL EDITORS OF THE COMMENTARY – NICHOLAS OKOH, VINAY SAMUEL AND CHRIS SUGDEN

The Latimer Trust

Participants in the Theological Resource Group meetings in Lagos, Oxford, Jerusalem and Uganda

Archbishop Nicholas Okoh (Nigeria - Chairman)
Canon Vinay Samuel (India - Convenor)
Revd Dr Mark Thompson (Australia)
Bishop Robinson Cavalcanti (Brazil)
Revd Dr Roger Beckwith (England)
Bishop Michael Nazir Ali (England)
Revd Dr Mike Ovey (England)
Mr Hugh Pratt (England)
Canon Dr Chris Sugden (England - secretary)
Revd Dr Joseph Galgalo (Kenya)
Revd Dr Emily Onyango (Kenya)
Archbishop Eliud Wabukala (Kenya)
Bishop Simeon Adebola (Nigeria)
Bishop John Akao (Nigeria)
Archdeacon Dr Dapu Asaju (Nigeria)
Bishop Michael Fape (Nigeria)
Bishop Ikechi Nwosu (Nigeria)
Dr Mrs A.O. Odunaiya (Nigeria)
Dr Mrs Ngozi Okeke (Nigeria)
Archbishop Bennett Okoro (Nigeria)
Bishop David Onuoha (Nigeria)
Professor George Malek (South Africa)
Dr Laurent Mbanda (Rwanda)
Bishop John Rucyahana (Rwanda)
Dr Paul Ntukumazina (Rwanda)
Archdeacon Moses Chin (South East Asia)
Bishop P.J. Lawrence (Church of South India)
Bishop Joel Obetia (Uganda)
Bishop Nicodemus Okille (Uganda)
Revd Dr Kevin Francis Donlan (USA/Rwanda)
Dr Stephen Noll (USA/Uganda)
Revd Dr Tudor Griffiths (Wales)
Bishop Dr Festus Yeboah-Asuamah (West Africa)
Mrs Sarah Finch (England - editor)

Advisory Group

Revd Jonathan Baker (England)
Revd Dr Gerald Bray (England - Latimer Trust)
Bishop Andrew Burnham (England)
Bishop John Ellison (England/Paraguay)
Canon Alistair Macdonald-Radcliff (England/Egypt)
Dr Lisa Nolland (England)
Revd Charles Raven (England)
Bishop Gideon Githiga (Kenya)
Dr John Senyonyi (Uganda)

CONTENTS

Foreword

The Most Revd Peter Jensen, Archbishop of Sydney
Secretary, Fellowship of Confessing Anglicans

I commend this commentary as an approved explication of the Jerusalem Declaration, and I commend it to the Anglican Communion for further discernment.

It is a contribution to the teaching ministry of the church for the equipping of all the people of God for ministry. I am delighted that the Church of Nigeria has already incorporated the Jerusalem Declaration into its prayer book. I am sure that, as the GAFCON Statement and the Declaration are increasingly referred to as a canon of contemporary faithfulness to the Scriptures, the commentary will become a key resource for churches.

For further information on:

o   The Fellowship of Confessing Anglicans and its regional expressions, and to identify with the *Statement on the Global Anglican Future* and join the Fellowship, please consult the website www.fca.net, email membership@gafcon.org, or write to The Secretariat, Fellowship of Confessing Anglicans, PO Box Q190, QVB Post Office, NSW 1230, Australia.

o   The Fellowship of Confessing Anglicans Theological Resource Group, please contact The Secretary, 21 High Street, Eynsham, OX29 4HE, UK, fcatrg@gmail.com.

Uniform with this volume: *The Way of the Cross: Biblical Resources for a Global Anglican Future* edited by Vinay Samuel – a six-week study course based on the Bible Studies at the Global Anglican Future Conference, Jerusalem 2008. The Latimer Trust 2009. ISBN 978-0-946307-98-2

STATEMENT ON THE GLOBAL ANGLICAN FUTURE

Praise the LORD!

It is good to sing praises to our God; for he is gracious, and a song of praise is fitting.

The LORD builds up Jerusalem; he gathers the outcasts of Israel. (Psalm 147:1-2)

Brothers and Sisters in Christ: We, the participants in the Global Anglican Future Conference, send you greetings from Jerusalem!

1. Introduction

The Global Anglican Future Conference (GAFCON), which was held in Jerusalem from 22-29 June 2008, is a spiritual movement to preserve and promote the truth and power of the gospel of salvation in Jesus Christ as we Anglicans have received it. The movement is *global:* it has mobilised Anglicans from around the world. We are *Anglican:* 1148 lay and clergy participants, including 291 bishops representing millions of faithful Anglican Christians. We cherish our Anglican heritage and the Anglican Communion and have no intention of departing from it. And we believe that, in God's providence, Anglicanism has a *bright future* in obedience to our Lord's Great Commission to make disciples of all nations and to build up the church on the foundation of biblical truth (Matthew 28:18-20; Ephesians 2:20).

GAFCON is not just a moment in time, but a movement in the Spirit, and we hereby:

❖ launch the GAFCON movement as a fellowship of confessing Anglicans

❖ publish the Jerusalem Declaration as the basis of the fellowship

❖ encourage GAFCON Primates to form a Council.

2. The Global Anglican Context

The future of the Anglican Communion is but a piece of the wider scenario of opportunities and challenges for the gospel in 21st century global culture. We rejoice in the way God has opened doors for gospel mission among many peoples, but we grieve for the spiritual decline in the most economically developed nations, where the forces of militant secularism and pluralism are eating away the fabric of society and churches are compromised and enfeebled in their witness. The vacuum left by them is readily filled by other faiths and deceptive cults. To meet these challenges will require Christians to work together to understand and oppose these forces and to liberate those under their sway. It will entail the planting of new churches among unreached peoples and also committed action to restore authentic Christianity to compromised churches.

The Anglican Communion, present in six continents, is well positioned to address this challenge, but currently it is divided and distracted. The Global Anglican Future Conference merged in response to a crisis within the Anglican Communion, a crisis involving *three undeniable facts* concerning world Anglicanism.

The first fact is the acceptance and promotion within the provinces of the Anglican Communion of a different 'gospel' (cf. Galatians 1:6-8) which is contrary to the apostolic gospel. This false gospel undermines the authority of God's Word written and the uniqueness of Jesus Christ as the author of salvation from sin, death and judgement. Many of its proponents claim that all religions offer equal access to God and that Jesus is only a way, not the way, the

3

truth and the life. It promotes a variety of sexual preferences and immoral behaviour as a universal human right. It claims God's blessing for same-sex unions over against the biblical teaching on holy matrimony. In 2003 this false gospel led to the consecration of a bishop living in a homosexual relationship.

The second fact is the declaration by provincial bodies in the Global South that they are out of communion with bishops and churches that promote this false gospel. These declarations have resulted in a realignment whereby faithful Anglican Christians have left existing territorial parishes, dioceses and provinces in certain Western churches and become members of other dioceses and provinces, all within the Anglican Communion. These actions have also led to the appointment of new Anglican bishops set over geographic areas already occupied by other Anglican bishops. A major realignment has occurred and will continue to unfold.

The third fact is the manifest failure of the Communion Instruments to exercise discipline in the face of overt heterodoxy. The Episcopal Church USA and the Anglican Church of Canada, in proclaiming this false gospel, have consistently defied the 1998 Lambeth statement of biblical moral principle (Resolution 1.10). Despite numerous meetings and reports to and from the 'Instruments of Unity,' no effective action has been taken, and the bishops of these unrepentant churches are welcomed to Lambeth 2008. To make matters worse, there has been a failure to honour promises of discipline, the authority of the Primates' Meeting has been undermined and the Lambeth Conference has been structured so as to avoid any hard decisions. We can only come to the devastating conclusion that 'we are a global Communion with a colonial structure'.

Sadly, this crisis has torn the fabric of the Communion in such a way that it cannot simply be patched back together. At the same time, it has brought together many Anglicans across the globe into personal and pastoral relationships in a fellowship which is faithful to biblical teaching, more representative of the demographic distribution of global Anglicanism today and stronger as an instrument of effective mission, ministry and social involvement.

3. A Fellowship of Confessing Anglicans

We, the participants in the Global Anglican Future Conference, are a fellowship of confessing Anglicans for the benefit of the Church and the furtherance of its mission. We are a *fellowship* of people united in the communion (*koinonia*) of the one Spirit and committed to work and pray together in the common mission of Christ. It is a *confessing* fellowship in that its members confess the faith of Christ crucified, stand firm for the gospel in the global and Anglican context, and affirm a contemporary rule, the Jerusalem Declaration, to guide the movement for the future. We are a fellowship of *Anglicans*, including provinces, dioceses, churches, missionary jurisdictions, para-church organisations and individual Anglican Christians whose goal is to reform, heal and revitalise the Anglican Communion and expand its mission to the world.

Our fellowship is not breaking away from the Anglican Communion. We, together with many other faithful Anglicans throughout the world, believe the doctrinal foundation of Anglicanism, which defines our core identity as Anglicans, is expressed in these words:

> The doctrine of the Church is grounded in the Holy Scriptures and in such teachings of the ancient Fathers and Councils of the Church as are agreeable to the said Scriptures. In particular, such doctrine is to be found in the Thirty-nine Articles of Religion, the Book of Common Prayer and the Ordinal.

We intend to remain faithful to this standard, and we call on others in the Communion to reaffirm and return to it. While acknowledging the nature of Canterbury as an historic see, we do not accept that Anglican identity is determined necessarily through recognition by the Archbishop of Canterbury. Building on the above doctrinal foundation of Anglican identity, we hereby publish the Jerusalem Declaration as the basis of our fellowship.

4. The Jerusalem Declaration

In the name of God the Father, God the Son and God the Holy Spirit:

We, the participants in the Global Anglican Future Conference, have met in the land of Jesus' birth. We express our loyalty as disciples to the King of kings, the Lord Jesus. We joyfully embrace his command to proclaim the reality of his kingdom which he first announced in this land. The gospel of the kingdom is the good news of salvation, liberation and transformation for all. In light of the above, we agree to chart a way forward together that promotes and protects the biblical gospel and mission to the world, solemnly declaring the following tenets of orthodoxy which underpin our Anglican identity.

1. We rejoice in the gospel of God through which we have been saved by grace through faith in Jesus Christ by the power of the Holy Spirit. Because God first loved us, we love him and as believers bring forth fruits of love, ongoing repentance, lively hope and thanksgiving to God in all things.

2. We believe the Holy Scriptures of the Old and New Testaments to be the word of God written and to contain all things necessary for salvation. The Bible is to be translated, read, preached, taught and obeyed in its plain and canonical sense, respectful of the Church's historic and consensual reading.

3. We uphold the four Ecumenical Councils and the three historic Creeds as expressing the rule of faith of the one holy catholic and apostolic Church.

4. We uphold the Thirty-nine Articles as containing the true doctrine of the Church agreeing with God's word and as authoritative for Anglicans today.

5. We gladly proclaim and submit to the unique and universal Lordship of Jesus Christ, the Son of God, humanity's only Saviour from sin, judgement and hell, who lived the life we could not live and died the death that we deserve. By his atoning death and glorious resurrection, he secured the redemption of all who come to him in repentance and faith.

6. We rejoice in our Anglican sacramental and liturgical heritage as an expression of the gospel, and we uphold the 1662 Book of Common Prayer as a true and authoritative standard of worship and prayer, to be translated and locally adapted for each culture.

7. We recognise that God has called and gifted bishops, priests and deacons in historic succession to equip all the people of God for their ministry in the world. We uphold the classic Anglican Ordinal as an authoritative standard of clerical orders.

8. We acknowledge God's creation of humankind as male and female and the unchangeable standard of Christian marriage between one man and one woman as the proper place for sexual intimacy and the basis of the family. We repent of our failures to maintain this standard and call for a renewed commitment to lifelong fidelity in marriage and abstinence for those who are not married.

9. We gladly accept the Great Commission of the risen Lord to make disciples of all nations, to seek those who do not know Christ and to baptise, teach and bring new believers to maturity.

10. We are mindful of our responsibility to be good stewards of God's creation, to uphold and advocate justice in society, and to seek relief and empowerment of the poor and needy.

11. We are committed to the unity of all those who know and love Christ and to building authentic ecumenical relationships. We recognise the orders and jurisdiction of those Anglicans who uphold orthodox faith and practice, and we encourage them to join us in this declaration.

12. We celebrate the God-given diversity among us which enriches our global fellowship, and we acknowledge freedom in secondary matters. We pledge to work together to seek the mind of Christ on issues that divide us.

13. We reject the authority of those churches and leaders who have denied the orthodox faith in word or deed. We pray for them and call on them to repent and return to the Lord.

14. We rejoice at the prospect of Jesus' coming again in glory, and while we await this final event of history, we praise him for the way he builds up his Church through his Spirit by miraculously changing lives.

5. The Road Ahead

We believe the Holy Spirit has led us during this week in Jerusalem to begin a new work. There are many important decisions for the development of this fellowship which will take more time, prayer and deliberation.

Among other matters, we shall seek to expand participation in this fellowship beyond those who have come to Jerusalem, including cooperation with the Global South and the Council of Anglican Provinces in Africa. We can, however, discern certain milestones on the road ahead.

6. Primates' Council

We, the participants in the Global Anglican Future Conference, do hereby acknowledge the participating Primates of GAFCON who have called us together, and encourage them to form the initial Council of the GAFCON movement. We look forward to the enlargement of the Council and entreat the Primates to organize and expand the fellowship of confessing Anglicans.

We urge the Primates' Council to authenticate and recognise confessing Anglican jurisdictions, clergy and congregations and to encourage all Anglicans to promote the gospel and defend the faith.

We recognise the desirability of territorial jurisdiction for provinces and dioceses of the Anglican Communion, except in those areas where churches and leaders are denying the orthodox faith or are preventing its spread, and in a few areas for which overlapping jurisdictions are beneficial for historical or cultural reasons.

We thank God for the courageous actions of those Primates and provinces who have offered orthodox oversight to churches under false leadership, especially in North and South America. The actions of these Primates have been a positive response to pastoral necessities and mission opportunities. We believe that such actions will continue to be necessary and we support them in offering help around the world.

We believe this is a critical moment when the Primates' Council will need to put in place structures to lead and support the church. In particular, we believe the time is now ripe for the formation of a province in North America for the federation currently known as Common Cause Partnership to be recognised by the Primates' Council.

7. Conclusion: Message from Jerusalem

We, the participants in the Global Anglican Future Conference, were summoned by the Primates' leadership team to Jerusalem in June 2008 to deliberate on the crisis that has divided the Anglican Communion for the past decade and to seek direction for the future. We have visited holy sites, prayed together, listened to God's Word preached and expounded, learned from various speakers and teachers, and shared our thoughts and hopes with each other.

The meeting in Jerusalem this week was called in a sense of urgency that a false gospel has so paralysed the Anglican Communion that this crisis must be addressed. The chief threat of this dispute involves the compromising of the integrity of the church's worldwide mission. The primary reason we have come to Jerusalem and issued this declaration is to free our churches to give clear and certain witness to Jesus Christ.

It is our hope that this Statement on the Global Anglican Future will be received with comfort and joy by many Anglicans around the world who have been distressed about the direction of the Communion. We believe the Anglican Communion should and will be reformed around the biblical gospel and mandate to go into all the world and present Christ to the nations.

Jerusalem
Feast of St Peter and St Paul
29 June 2008

Introduction to the Statement on the Global Anglican Future

1. How did the Anglican Communion come to be so seriously divided?

How did the worldwide Anglican Communion come to the present situation, in which its conflict is a matter of continual public debate, and where it seems no peace-initiatives have been able to succeed? How did the Communion come to be so divided that some provinces have declared impaired communion, and have even broken communion, with the two provinces in North America? The fact that, in the summer of 2008, there were *two* international conferences of bishops taking place, the Lambeth Conference and GAFCON (Global Anglican Future Conference), reflects the seriousness of the issues we are facing.

Some of us who met at GAFCON have watched these events for well over a decade, and have been involved in several attempts to avert and end the crisis. These efforts have been summarized by Archbishop Peter Akinola who, as Chairman of GAFCON, Chairman of the Global South and, at that time, Chairman of the Council of Anglican Provinces of Africa, bore a great sense of responsibility for the welfare of the whole Communion. He has written on this at length in 'A Most Agonizing Journey towards Lambeth 2008'[1] which we summarize here.

He writes:

We have been on this journey for ten long years. It has been costly and debilitating for all concerned, as demonstrated most recently by the tepid response to the invitations to the proposed Lambeth Conference 2008. At a time when we should be able to gather together and celebrate remarkable stories of growth, and the many wonderful ways in which our God has been at work in our beloved Communion, with

---

[1] In *The Way, the Truth and the Life: Theological Resources for a Pilgrimage to a Global Anglican Future* (London, Latimer Trust, 2008), reprinted in full below p. 71

lives being transformed, new churches being built and new dioceses established, there is little enthusiasm even to meet. There are continual cries for patience, listening and understanding. And yet the record shows that those who hold to the "faith once and for all delivered to the saints" have shown remarkable forbearance, while their pleas have been ignored, their leaders have been demonized, and their advocates marginalized.

He traces the steps of this journey:

In February 1997 in Kuala Lumpur, during the 2nd Encounter of the Global South Anglican Communion, a statement was issued expressing concern about the apparent setting aside of biblical teaching by some provinces and dioceses.

The 1998 Lambeth Conference issued Resolution 1.10. This affirmed the teaching of the Holy Scriptures with regard to faithfulness in marriage between a man and a woman in lifelong union, and declared that homosexual practice was incompatible with biblical teaching. This decision was supported by an overwhelming majority of the bishops of the Communion.

In March 2000, at their meeting in Oporto, Portugal, the Primates reaffirmed the supremacy of Scripture as the 'decisive authority in the life of our Communion'.

In 2001, the Primates' Meeting in Kanuga, North Carolina, issued a pastoral letter acknowledging estrangement in the church, due to changes in theology and practice regarding human sexuality, and calling on all provinces of the Communion to avoid actions that might damage the 'credibility of mission in the world'.

In April 2002, after their meeting at Canterbury, the Primates issued a further pastoral letter, recognising the responsibility of all bishops to articulate the fundamentals of faith and maintain Christian truth.

In October 2002, the twelfth meeting of the Anglican Consultative Council took place in Hong Kong, and a resolution [34] was approved that urged dioceses and bishops to refrain from unilateral actions and policies that would strain communion.

In July/August 2003, at the ECUSA General Convention in Minneapolis, the delegates chose, among their many actions, to reject a Resolution [B001] that affirmed the authority of Scripture and other basic elements of Christian faith. They also approved the election of someone living in an unashamedly sexual relationship outside marriage, in this case a non-celibate same-sex relationship, as a bishop.

The Primates' Meeting[2] specially convened at Lambeth Palace, in October 2003, issued a pastoral statement condemning ECUSA's decisions at General Convention, describing them as actions that 'threaten the unity of our own Communion as well as our relationships with other parts of Christ's Church, our mission and witness, and our relations with other faiths, in a world already confused in areas of sexuality, morality and theology and polarized Christian opinion.' They also declared that if the consecration (of the man elected to be bishop) proceeded 'the future of the Communion itself will be put in jeopardy', and that the action would 'tear the fabric of our communion at its deepest level, and may lead to further division on this and further issues as provinces have to decide in consequence whether they can remain in communion with provinces that choose not to break communion with the

---

[2] Dr Colin Podmore writes in 'The Governance of the Church of England and the Anglican Communion' (Church of England General Synod Paper GS Misc 910: www.cofe.anglican.org/about/gensynod/agendas/feb09/gsmisc910.pdf), pp.15-18:

4.17 ... in 1978 Archbishop [Donald] Coggan re-established a separate 'Primates' Meeting' [a meeting of the senior bishops of each church]. ... [He said that] the primates should meet 'reasonably often, for leisurely thought, prayer, and deep consultation... perhaps as frequently as once in two years'. The primates would be 'the channels through which the voice of the member churches would be heard, and real interchange of heart could take place'. Secondly, the Primates Meeting should 'be in the very closest and intimate contact with the Anglican Consultative Council' [Report of the Lambeth Conference 1978, pp. 122-124]. Thus Archbishop Coggan explicitly saw the establishment of the Primates Meeting as part of a solution to the question of authority in the Anglican Communion....

4.25 The Primates' Meeting, by contrast, is an episcopal body and its members are by definition those who pre-eminently speak on behalf of their own churches. As the Virginia report put it, 'Their meetings have an inherent authority by virtue of the office which they hold as chief pastors' [The Official Report of the Lambeth Conference 1998, p.61]. ... A statement made by the Primates' Meeting is a statement by a meeting whose members have an inherent authority by virtue of their episcopal ordination and of the offices that they hold in their individual churches. It thus carries significant weight, but not the same weight as a resolution of the episcopate of the Communion as a whole.

Episcopal Church (USA)'. They also called on 'the provinces concerned to make adequate provision for Episcopal oversight of dissenting minorities within their own area of pastoral care in consultation with the Archbishop of Canterbury on behalf of the Primates'.

ECUSA responded, the following month, by proceeding with the consecration of Gene Robinson, thereby tearing the fabric of our Communion and forcing the Church of Nigeria, along with many other provinces, to sever communion with ECUSA.

One of the consequences of this continuing intransigence by ECUSA was the alienation of thousands of faithful Anglicans who make their home in the USA. The attempts by the Primates to provide for their protection, through the Panel of Reference, proved fruitless.

So, the desire of these faithful Anglicans for an alternative spiritual home led to many impassioned requests to the Church of Nigeria, and also to a number of other provinces within the Global South. The Standing Committee of the Church of Nigeria recognised this urgent need during their meeting in Ilesa in March 2004 and, as a result, initiated a process for the provision of pastoral care through the formation of a Convocation within the USA. As a matter of courtesy, the Archbishop of Canterbury was duly informed of these intentions. The Churches of Rwanda, Kenya, Uganda and Southern Cone have provided similar oversight.

The *Windsor Report*, released in September 2004, reaffirmed Lambeth Resolution 1.10, and also the authority of Scripture as being central to Anglican Common Life. The Windsor Report also called for three moratoria, one on public rites of same-sex blessing, another on the election to the episcopate, and consent, of any candidate who was living in a same-sex union, and a third on the provision of pastoral oversight for those in dispute with their bishop.

During the African Anglican Bishops Conference (AABC), in October 2004, the Primates who were present released a statement which, among other things, urged the Episcopal Church USA and the Anglican Church of Canada to take seriously the need for 'repentance, forgiveness and reconciliation enjoined on all Christians by Christ'. It called on these two churches to move beyond informal expressions of regret for the effect of their actions, and to have a genuine change of heart and mind.

Although, at their meeting in The Dromantine, Northern Ireland in February 2005, the Primates had advised the withdrawal of both ECUSA and the ACoC from the Anglican Consultative Council, the continued influence of these churches on the Communion, and their renewed efforts to cause others to adopt their intransigent line, frustrated any genuine attempts at reconciliation.

The Third Anglican South-to-South Encounter, meeting in Egypt in October 2005, issued a very strong indictment of ECUSA and the ACoC, and called for a common 'Anglican Covenant' among churches remaining true to biblical Christianity and historic Anglicanism. Despite all the calls for repentance, the blessing of homosexual unions, and the nominating of practising homosexuals to the episcopacy, continued in the USA.

The Global South Anglican Primates, meeting in Kigali in September 2006, recognised that ECUSA appeared to have no intention of changing direction and once again embracing the 'faith once delivered'. In their communiqué they wrote: 'We are convinced that the time has now come to take initial steps towards the formation of what will be recognised as a separate ecclesiastical structure of the Anglican Communion in the USA ... We believe that we would be failing in our apostolic witness if we do not make this provision for those who hold firmly to a commitment to historic Anglican faith.'

They also stated, in *The Road to Lambeth*: 'We Anglicans stand at a crossroads. One road, the road of compromise of biblical truth, leads to destruction and disunity. The other road has its own obstacles [faithfulness is never an easy way] because it requires changes in the way the Communion has been governed and it challenges [all] our churches to live up to and into their full maturity in Christ.' Further, they warned that if Gene Robinson and those who consented to his election and participated in his consecration were present at the 2008 Lambeth Conference, they would not be able to attend.[3][4]

The Anglican Communion Primates, meeting in Dar es Salaam in February 2007, reaffirmed the 1998 Lambeth Resolution 1:10 and called on ECUSA (now renamed The Episcopal Church, TEC) to consider definite actions, which could heal the Communion as well as reassure those who had been deprived of adequate pastoral care. The Primates set a deadline of 30 September, by which date they hoped to have a response. By June 2007, both the ACoC and TEC had indicated an unwillingness to comply with these requests, but had expressed a desire to remain part of the Communion they had hurt so much. The Primates' deadline came, and went; it was ignored.

The situation was made even more incoherent by the decision, made in July 2007, to extend an invitation to the Lambeth Conference to those responsible for this crisis, with no accompanying call to repentance, but not to invite certain bishops who have stood firm for the faith.

Apart from these gatherings, at which attempts to address the issue were made in a spirit of humility and with a deep commitment to the unity of the Communion, senior GAFCON Primates took the initiative to travel to England to meet with the Archbishop of Canterbury on 5 December 2008, in order to encourage decisive actions which would maintain the faith, protect the faithful and discipline those who had walked away from the faith.

Yet, none of these attempts was able to contain or reverse the breakdown. Why has this been the case?

Our perception is that, in their necessary attempt to address the rapidly changing and complex cultural challenges that they faced, churches in large sections of the West have allowed culture to dominate their church's belief and behaviour. Since the governance

---

[3] http://www.globalsouthanglican.org/index.php/comments/
the_road_to_lambeth_ presented_at_capa.
[4] See Romans 1:32, '... but also approve of those who practise them.' The bishops who had consecrated Gene Robinson had demonstrated that they approved his practice.

of the Communion is largely centred on London and those who live in the West, this same culture has dominated the response of the leadership of the Communion.

2. What is the nature of these cultural challenges?

Postmodern culture, a major force in the West, may be described as a culture of repudiation and innovation, using an analogy suggested by Roger Scruton in *Culture Counts: Faith and Feeling in a World Beseiged.*[5]

Scruton describes the culture of repudiation as follows:

o   It repudiates the belief that reason can lead to objective truth.

o   Appeal to reason is only to a Western way of thinking and is not universal. Reason conceals oppression.

o   Truth is not absolute but a product of debate. As arguments change so does truth.

o   Every thought and idea comes from a context and context is more important than the idea.

o   Traditional (orthodox) views of personhood, family, sexual relations and sexual morality have no authority as truth but can only be viewed as an opinion.

o   It repudiates the possibility of the universal. Only the multicultural is possible. Reason cannot be a universal category. Universal categories even if they exist are not accessible. So no universal demands can be made of any culture. A universal human nature is a myth.

o   In place of objectivity we have 'inter-subjectivity' – in other words consensus. Truth, meanings, facts and values are all negotiable. Negotiation takes the place of rational agreement. We can each tell our stories and begin to negotiate how we can move together or apart.

---

[5] Roger Scruton, *Culture Counts: Faith and Feeling in a World Beseiged* (New York: Encounter, 2007).

o   It is absolute relativism except that it excludes all conservatives and traditionalists as reactionary.

Scruton describes the culture of innovation as follows:

o   The key drive of contemporary culture is the future, which humans must shape. The past is at best a background and may be a resource for the future.

o   We do not plan the future. We create it. It is a 'Pure Future'. It is an individual search for spirituality, for meaning, creating something out of many fragments and continually innovating. It exalts a view of a human being as not only a reflective being but also an agent who has the capacity and drive to work on and transform the world.

Against such cultural drives of repudiation and innovation, those with more traditional views find it difficult to find a language for dialogue, let alone reach a common ground.

3. How has this culture impacted the Communion?

A significant number of senior leaders in the Anglican Communion have been shaped, influenced and even trapped by this culture of repudiation and innovation. They have allowed the influence of this culture to intimidate them and, in the face of this pressure, have attempted to show the relevance of Christian faith with innovations of their own. Some have gone so far as to discern the activity of the Holy Spirit in the drives of this culture and its expressions in people's lives, against the plain and express teaching of Scripture, which is relegated to the archives of patriarchy. Their actions are witness to the fact that, in their faith and practice, they are overturning the authority of the Scriptures as understood in Anglican teaching. For example, the *Pilling Report* in the Church of England identified in 2007 that the selection process of bishops was unfairly loaded against those with clear convictions, in favour of compromise candidates.

Some churches in the West, and most in the Global South, have resisted the impact of this culture of repudiation and innovation for the most part. This may be because their members have yet to face its full impact, but it may also be because, in these people's experience, faithfulness to the received faith has enabled their churches to grow; they have seen transformation in people's personal lives and also in communities. They see no need to abandon the received gospel in favour of innovations, because the received gospel is able to respond adequately to the challenges of contemporary society in all its various forms.

4. What was the tipping point?

Those who had struggled with these issues for well over a decade, recognised that the crunch point had come, in July 2007, when the invitations to the Lambeth Conference were sent out. The sole functioning Instrument of the Communion at that time, the Archbishop of Canterbury invited the consecrators of Gene Robinson to come and share fellowship with the rest of the bishops, despite the fact that a third of the Communion had publicly broken relationships with these consecrating bishops. When The Episcopal Church consecrated Gene Robinson as bishop, and when no effective discipline followed, orthodox Primates and provinces had declared that they and their churches were out of communion with those who had consecrated Gene Robinson, and had appealed for a postponement of the Lambeth Conference until the issue could be resolved. However, the Archbishop of Canterbury decided, after inadequate consultation, to press ahead with inviting all the TEC Bishops to Lambeth.[6] As a result, 230 bishops declined the invitation to the Lambeth Conference.

We perceive that the situation is like that of a family, with a child that is being favoured and a child that is being abused. Child A is allowed to behave as it wishes. Child B suffers from that abuse and appeals to the head of the family. However, the father of the family decides to call both children to come back together to live in fellowship, without dealing with the abuse. When Child B refuses to come to live in such fellowship, the reputation of the father and the

---

[6] *The Road to Lambeth* had said that the issue was to be solved before Lambeth could take place, and the Primates were supposed to meet following the deadline of 30 September 2007. See 'The Decline and Fall (and Rising Again) of the Anglican Communion', an address given to the Mere Anglicanism Conference on 16 January 2009: http://www.stephenswitness.com/2009/01/decline-and-fall-and-rising-again-of.html.

family is said to be at stake.

So Lambeth was organized primarily to show that the father of the family still had authority (though it appeared to have little content), and that the family was still harmonious. The Lambeth Conference was intended to reinforce the authority of the Archbishop of Canterbury and to rescue the reputation of the Anglican Communion in the eyes of the world. It was to be an exercise in control rather than of leadership.

Some orthodox bishops, acting with integrity and an honest commitment to the truth, attended the Lambeth Conference out of a concern to bear witness to that truth in the face of other views that would be represented, and to participate in a recognition of mutual accountability. Several found that that the conference was designed, not as a neutral space for reflection, but as a way of avoiding the problem.[7] It was at best only a time for mutual sharing, without any call for mutual accountability.

In situations such as the present crisis, different positions will only be heard and taken seriously when there is a recognition that a serious problem needs to be addressed. However, when there is denial that any serious problem exists, the attempt to present an orthodox position is futile. As a result, those who had gone to Lambeth to bear witness were driven to issue statements of disassociation and frustration as the conference ended. Lambeth 2008 had become yet another example of how the culture of denial allows innovation without accountability.

Furthermore, the conference was immediately followed by

---

[7] The following statements are listed in the order of their appearance.
Church of Sudan's statement to the Lambeth Conference:
http://www.anglican-mainstream.net/?p=4386;
Presiding Bishop Mouneer Anis: http://www.anglican-mainstream.net/?p=4592;
Global South Primates: http://www.globalsouthanglican.org/index.php/comments/
statement_on_lambeth_conference_2008;
The Bishop of Winchester's report on the Lambeth Conference:
http://www.winchester.anglican.org/page.php?id=1485;
Bishop Harrower of Tasmania's report: http://www.anglican-mainstream.net/?p=5329;
Bishop Richard Ellena of Nelson, Aotearoa/New Zealand: http://www.standfirminfaith.com
/index.php/site/article/15066.

further acts by heterodox bishops, such as the deposition of the Bishop of Pittsburgh.

Those who called GAFCON discerned that this would be the trajectory of events, given the power of the culture of repudiation and denial. Out of concern for the very future of the Anglican Communion, they decided to seek counsel, to pray, and to return to their biblical and historical roots in the Holy Land, in a coalition of the willing. And this at a time when those in the Communion who had been given the responsibility to act had in fact done nothing.

5. How did GAFCON respond to the failure of discipline?

The GAFCON Statement, which contains the Jerusalem Declaration, is a prophetic response to the current situation of indiscipline. In the Old Testament, prophets emerged when the priests and kings failed to express the will, love and discipline of God in the community of Israel.

The Global Anglican Future Conference in Jerusalem, in June 2008, had been called by a number of Primates, who invited fellow bishops, other clergy and laity to take counsel with them. The prophetic action of issuing the GAFCON Statement, with the Jerusalem Declaration, produced two responses to the current situation.

The first response was that this conference urged the GAFCON Primates to form a Primates' Council (GPC), to do what the Communion Primates' Meeting (CPM) had undertaken to do but had failed to do: restore order in the Communion.

The GAFCON Primates' Council is an initiative of governance and unity in the Anglican Communion, to deal with the problems that the Instruments have shown themselves unable to address, and to revitalize and reposition the role of Primates in the Communion.

The Primates' Council was formed to exercise these Primates' authority as metropolitans and to recognise those who are authentic Anglicans. It is intended that the Primates' Council provide a *de facto* pastoral forum. This is to be a framework for communion and oversight for orthodox Anglicans who do not wish to remain in fellowship with those who have persistently transgressed the teachings and practice of the Anglican Communion, which itself continues to be faithful to biblical teaching. There is no need to be precisely canonical at this stage, since every canonical framework has a history of moral authority over time before it is formalized in canonical systems.

The GAFCON Primates' Council has been encouraged to recognise and affirm the Common Cause Partnership Province in North America. The main circumstance that contributed to this action was the Archbishop of Canterbury's proposals to provide help to the orthodox in TEC which were flawed because they maintained communion with those who had abandoned the orthodox faith. These proposals were:

1. the Panel of Reference,

2. the proposals for Delegated Pastoral Oversight, unacceptable to the orthodox Anglicans in the United States, and

3. the Pastoral Forum, proposed at the 2008 Lambeth Conference, which was established without any consultation with those for whom it was intended.

As a second and distinct response, the GAFCON Statement says that the participants in GAFCON 'are a fellowship of confessing Anglicans for the benefit of the Church and the furtherance of its mission.' The Fellowship of Confessing Anglicans (FCA) stands in the tradition of the voluntary principle in the Anglican Communion, whereby members of formal structures (parishes, dioceses and provinces) can at the same time form sodalities to further the mission of the Church. Such sodalities are well known in the Catholic tradition, just as voluntary societies have been a long-standing feature of the evangelical tradition. FCA was intentionally designed as a fellowship within the Anglican Communion, not a church within a church governed by a Primates' Council.

6. Why 'Confessing Anglicans'?

Over against the culture of repudiation and innovation, public confession of the apostolic faith is necessary in order to shine the light in a dark place. To identify where orthodox Anglicans stand in response to these powerful cultural influences, it is necessary to confess that which we believe in relation to the current challenges. This is a time-honoured response of the Church to the challenges to its life. More importantly, it is an expression of, and a humble witness to, our orthodoxy and identity as Anglicans, living under the full and complete authority of the Bible. It is not a test of orthodoxy for all Anglicans. We are most emphatically not suggesting that those who do not subscribe to the same confession are thereby any less faithful Anglicans. We are not attempting to fix Anglican identity but to reaffirm it, as being anchored in the apostolic faith, and as belonging to a Christian church which is centred on the gospel and bounded by Scripture. We invite others who share this confession to stand with us.

Commentary on The Jerusalem Declaration

1.   The shape of The Jerusalem Declaration

The Declaration falls into two parts. In the first part, seven clauses refer to the classic authorities of Anglicanism – these have just been mentioned, in the section of the GAFCON Statement immediately preceding the Declaration – and they are: the Bible as the word of God written, the Creeds and Councils of the early church, the Articles of Religion, the Book of Common Prayer and the Ordinal. Though each of these appeared at particular moments of history, each one is recognised as having an ongoing normative role. The Bible stands above all the others, as the supreme authority for Christian faith and life, and the authority of each of the others stems from the fact that each one faithfully represents the teaching of Scripture. These, then, are the classic standards of Anglicanism, and they have never been superseded by others.

In the second part, seven clauses address particular matters that confront the churches today. Marriage and sexuality, mission, and the call to stand for social justice are all aspects of our life in the world at large. Our relations with other Anglicans and other Christians, our God-given diversity and the freedom that God gives so that this may be enjoyed, and the need for discipline and for prayer, for those within our fellowship and those outside it – these are matters which have to do more specifically with our life as the people of God. The Declaration ends on a note of hope, the hope of Christ's return in glory, while also recognising that the present transformative work of the Holy Spirit anticipates the kingdom to come.

2. The preamble

The Jerusalem Declaration begins with a preamble, followed by fourteen 'tenets of orthodoxy' which, the document insists, 'underpin our Anglican identity'.

> In the name of God the Father, God the Son and God the Holy Spirit:

This trinitarian opening of The Jerusalem Declaration is not simply a formality. The God who is known and proclaimed throughout the world, who gathers his people and who moved in us to bring us together in Jerusalem at this critical hour, is the triune God. God is not to be described, only or even principally, in terms of his activity, as Creator, for example, or Redeemer, or Sanctifier, but personally, in terms of his eternal relations: the Father, the Son, and the Spirit of the Father and the Son. He is personally and actively involved with his people now, just as he has always been. The mission given to the first disciples was to baptize the nations 'in the name of the Father and of the Son and of the Holy Spirit' (Matthew 28:19). We rejoice in the grace of the Lord Jesus Christ, and the love of God, and the fellowship of the Holy Spirit (2 Corinthians 13:14).

> *We, the participants in the Global Anglican Future Conference, have met in the land of Jesus' birth. We express our loyalty as disciples to the King of kings, the Lord Jesus. We joyfully embrace his command to proclaim the reality of his kingdom which he first announced in this land. The gospel of the kingdom is the good news of salvation, liberation and transformation for all. In the light of the above, we agree to chart a way forward together that promotes and protects the biblical gospel and mission to the world, solemnly declaring the following tenets of orthodoxy which underpin our Anglican identity.*

The honour of Jesus, the promised Messiah and the eternal Son of God (Romans 1:1-7), is the Declaration's principal concern. Therefore the purpose of the Declaration, which was composed in Jerusalem, is to call everyone who claims the name of Jesus to hear him and obey his words. The historical roots of our Christian faith, in both Old and New Testaments, are associated with the holy land and Jerusalem as with nowhere else. It is the land where Jesus was born, where he walked and taught his disciples and worked miracles. Jerusalem is the city of David, which Jesus entered on Palm Sunday, hailed as Messiah. Here, that same week, he was arrested, tried and crucified under Pontius Pilate. Here he was buried and rose victorious from the tomb on the third day, in fulfilment of the Scriptures (1 Corinthians 15:3-5). At the Mount of Olives he commissioned his apostles to make disciples of all nations (Matthew 28:18-20), and then ascended. The final kingdom, which he promises when he comes again in glory, is described as the New Jerusalem coming down from heaven (Revelation 21:2).

We are convinced that the Jesus of history and the Christ of faith are one and the same, and that the apostolic writings bear truthful testimony to his person and work. At a time when false gospels and imaginary Christs are being proclaimed in many parts of the world, and even in the Church, it is entirely appropriate and also highly symbolic to return to the holy land and Jerusalem, where the real Jesus himself first preached the gospel of the kingdom and called on men and women to repent and believe. The gospel message we have for the world is one of salvation, liberation and transformation through Jesus Christ and him alone. God has richly provided for us in Christ Jesus (Ephesians 1:3-14). Through him we have salvation from the judgement and wrath we deserve (1 Thessalonians 1:10), liberation from the powers which had enslaved us (Romans 6:6-7), and transformation from enemies of God to sons of God (Romans 5: 6-10; Galatians 4:3-7; Ephesians 2:1-10). In the gospel this message of deliverance is proclaimed, and all are invited to come and share in it.

The salvation that comes through Jesus is inseparably tied to his kingship. Jesus is Lord. Because he rules, all reality is determined by him. Our response to his lordship is critical – we need to recognise that the good news of salvation and the gospel of God's kingdom go together. Therefore, the appropriate response to his lordship is to repent and believe, to anticipate now the reality that will be unavoidable on the last day, when every knee will bow and every tongue confess that Jesus Christ is Lord, to the glory of God the Father (Philippians 2:10-11).

The kingdom that Jesus proclaimed has a corporate identity. The Church is the harbinger of the final kingdom, exposing the false ideologies of every age and showing forth the manifold wisdom of God (Ephesians 3:10). The apostolic Church is charged to maintain true doctrine, by which men and women are saved (1 Timothy 4:16). This doctrine has been recorded in Scripture and preserved through the faithful teaching of the Church in history. The Church's message is conveyed not only in word but also in deed, in the evidence of transformed lives and transformed relationships of love (John 13:35).

The aberrant behaviour, springing from aberrant belief, of some within the Anglican Communion has no doubt been the catalyst, but it is not the only reason why the GAFCON movement has been necessary. First and foremost it is the gospel imperative, the priority of mission in a world that is lurching towards its own destruction, which compels us to unite in this way. The gospel of Jesus Christ needs to be heard by all, so that as many as possible may be saved. When those who seek to proclaim this gospel are hindered from doing so, it is critical that faithful men and women should act to protect the integrity of the message, and also the freedom of the messengers to fulfil the commission that Jesus has given them. All that follows in The Jerusalem Declaration needs to be understood in the light of this fundamental commitment.

Clause 1: The gospel of God

We rejoice in the gospel of God through which we have been saved by grace through faith in Jesus Christ by the power of the Holy Spirit. Because God first loved us, we love him and as believers bring forth fruits of love, ongoing repentance, lively hope and thanksgiving to God in all things.

The gospel is God's message of salvation through Jesus Christ and, to those who receive it, it is glad tidings of great joy (Romans 1:3, 16-17; Luke 2:10). God has acted to save us by sending his Son to deal with sin and all its consequences (Romans 3:21-26). The gospel is the ultimate revelation and demonstration of God's love, a love which is beyond human devising and which does not wait for us to become lovely, but reaches out to us even while we are sinners and enemies of God, and sets us in the right with himself (1 Corinthians 2:5-10; Romans 5:1-11). This love is expressed principally in Jesus' sacrifice on the cross (see further Clause 5). We are saved by God's grace through faith, a faith which is itself a gift of God (Ephesians 2:8). That we are justified by faith is, as Article XI of the Thirty-nine Articles affirms, 'a most wholesome Doctrine, and very full of comfort'.

This salvation makes a difference in the everyday lives of those who are rescued. God does not simply add his blessing to patterns of life that have been embraced without him, or that are in opposition to his word. The same Spirit who unites us to Christ and gives us faith, now works in us to make us like Christ. He both challenges our preoccupation with ourselves and produces the fruit of godly living within us. He enables us to turn from our various idolatries (Colossians 3:5), to call God 'Father' (Romans 8:1-30) and to give thanks in all circumstances (1 Thessalonians 5:18). God is love, and he transforms us through his love, so that we may love him and love our neighbour as ourselves (1 John 4:9-19).

This clause is placed first because the critical reality of our lives as Christians is that we are redeemed people. Our lives are now lived in response to the mercy we have been shown, a mercy that is completely undeserved (Romans 12:1-2).

Clause 2: The Holy Scriptures

> We believe the Holy Scriptures of the Old and New Testaments to be the word of God written and to contain all things necessary for salvation. The Bible is to be translated, read, preached, taught and obeyed in its plain and canonical sense, respectful of the Church's historic and consensual reading.

The one true and living God who redeems us is an active and speaking God. By his word the world was made (Genesis 1:3, 6, 9, 11 etc.; Psalm 33:6). He spoke a word of blessing and command to the first man and woman in the Garden of Eden (Genesis 1:28-30; 2:16-17). Throughout the history of Israel, he made his purposes known through a long succession of prophets and, as the climax of that history, he has spoken to us by his Son (Hebrews 1:1-2). Whenever God speaks, his words command attention. His words are always active and powerful (Hebrews 4:12). They always accomplish their intended purpose (Isaiah 55:10-11).

Jesus Christ, the Word become flesh (John 1:1-14), himself acknowledged the Old Testament to be the written word of God, and appealed to its authority as decisive (e.g. Matthew 4:1-11; Mark 7:1-13; 10:1-12). He also commissioned his apostles to take his words to the ends of the earth, until the end of the age, and he promised them his Spirit to enable them to fulfil this Great Commission (Matthew

28:18-20; Acts 1:8; John 14:26; 16:5-15). In this way, the authority of Jesus stands behind the apostolic ministry which produced the New Testament, just as his authority gave continuing validity to the Old Testament as God's word to us. Contrary to the suggestions of some, we are never presented with a choice between following Jesus and obeying the teaching of Scripture.

The Scriptures are primarily a testimony to Jesus Christ (Luke 24:27; John 5:39). Both the Old Testament and the New Testament point us to him and to the salvation from sin, death and judgement that he has won for us. They reveal how we should respond to him and to all he has done. As John wrote about his Gospel, 'these are written that you may believe that Jesus is the Christ, the Son of God, and that by believing you may have life in his name' (John 20:31). The Scriptures are sufficient for the purpose for which they have been given: making known the God who saves, explaining how he saves, and directing us in how to live as those who have been saved (2 Timothy 3:14-15). This is what Article VI (of the Thirty-nine Articles) means when it says that the Holy Scripture contains 'all things necessary to salvation'.

The Bible is unique. While it is a book of human words, it is at the same time God-breathed Scripture. These are the very words which God wanted written for us. This is what we mean when we say that the Bible is 'inspired' (2 Timothy 3:16-17). The human writers were consciously and creatively involved in writing these words, but the end result is the written word of God, which comes to us through the work of the Spirit of God (2 Peter 1:20-21). It is this ultimate source in God that gives the Scriptures their special character. These are *holy* writings, distinct from all other human literature, and set apart as the special instrument of God's purpose (2 Timothy 3:15). So while fresh translations of these texts are necessary from time to time, the content of the texts is not to be tampered with, revised or set aside.

Nor can these texts be added to in any way. The early church recognised that the canon of Scripture is settled. The apostolic foundation has been laid and, with the death of the apostles, no group or individual has authority to add to it or remove from it. While there certainly was a process of careful investigation and thorough scrutiny of New Testament books in the first four centuries, none of the official letters or council decisions of that period was intended as an attempt to reconstitute the canon of Scripture. Rather, they were a recognition of a distinct and unique authority that was already characteristic of the writings of the apostles, and of those most closely associated with them, an authority which required that these texts be placed alongside 'the other Scriptures' (2 Peter 3:16).

While the various books of the Bible were produced in the midst of human history, they are not restricted by this history. They are not bound or conditioned by time. The teaching of Scripture remains as relevant and effective in the twenty-first century as it was in the first century. '... the grass withers and the flowers fall, but the word of the Lord stands for ever' (1 Peter 1:24-25). Nor is the teaching of Scripture bound by geography or culture. The biblical texts are translatable from the original languages for every culture. They are universally applicable and eternally relevant. Whatever the real and significant differences between us and the early Christians of the Mediterranean, to whom the apostolic writings were first addressed, we share with them a common created human nature and a common need of the salvation that only comes in Christ. Furthermore, we, like them, live in the last days. In this light, we insist that contextualisation does not mean modifying the Scripture to suit our culture; we should, instead, be bringing every aspect of our culture under the authority of Scripture.

The Bible is a clear and effective piece of communication. It can be read with confidence that its plain meaning is accessible. When it is read prayerfully, with due consideration of its context (in the paragraph, chapter, book and the whole of Scripture), the particular type of writing we are dealing with at each point (history, law, poetry, vision, letter, etc.), and the actual words that have been written (rather than what we think should have been said, or what we think has been left out), we can expect to understand it. After all, God does want us to know him and his purposes for us.

God has also given us all the resources necessary for understanding any part of Scripture properly. Three of these may be noted here. First, God has given us his Holy Spirit, the same Spirit whose work produced the Scriptures, to enable us to understand Scripture's meaning and its significance in our lives. Second, God has given us the whole Bible, not just a few isolated texts, so that what may appear unclear in one place is very often clarified when it is compared with what is said in other places. The Church is not free 'so [to] expound one place of Scripture, that it be repugnant to another' (Article XX of the Thirty-nine Articles). Finally and critically, God has given us each other with our various gifts. Reading the Bible together can help us avoid simply reading our own preferences, or those of our culture, into the biblical text.

As a piece of communication, Scripture has a definite meaning. God has not been evasive or ambiguous; he has something specific to say to his people by means of the Scriptures. Our task, as responsible readers, is to pay careful attention to the text, with the help of the resources we have been given, in order to understand what has been written. The suggestion that all we can expect from reading Scripture is a possible 'interpretation', one which must not under any circumstances be privileged above any other 'interpretation', fails to take seriously the fact that God is active in making himself and his purposes known. Different readings need to be tested against the text of Scripture itself, with the humble acknowledgement that it may be our partial knowledge, our prejudices or our sinfulness that has led to a misreading. We must be willing to have our minds changed by the words that *God* has given to us. (See below, in the commentary on Clause 12 of The Jerusalem Declaration, for a discussion of the important concept of *adiaphora*, meaning those matters on which faithful obedience to Scripture allows room for freedom and diversity.)

We are part of a rich reading fellowship, stretching back over two thousand years. The Bible is not simply the possession of twenty-first century Anglicans, to do with as we please. Others have read the Scriptures before us and others are reading the Scriptures alongside us. We can benefit from listening to what they have had to say. In particular, we have much to gain from biblical scholarship, which is at its best when it is disciplined by faith and the Spirit (1 Corinthians 2:1-16). Our understanding of Scripture is enriched by the insights of faithful biblical scholarship but is not dependent upon them. After all, Scripture is not tested by biblical scholarship, but biblical scholarship must always be tested by Scripture, following the example of the Berean Christians, who examined the Scriptures daily 'to see if what Paul said was true' (Acts 17:11).

The Bible has always been central to the Christian life

because it is the word of God to us. It is impossible to take God seriously without taking seriously the words which he has spoken and which he caused to be written for us. This is the instrument that the Spirit of God uses to transform the lives of his people. The teaching of Scripture is also able to confront and transform society and culture. The word of God remains powerful. Today, as ever, it is 'living and active. Sharper than any double-edged sword, it penetrates even to dividing soul and spirit, joints and marrow; it judges the thoughts and attitudes of the heart' (Hebrews 4:12).

Clause 3: The rule of faith

> *We uphold the four Ecumenical Councils and the three historic Creeds as expressing the rule of faith of the one holy catholic and apostolic Church.*

While Scripture itself is supreme over all human formularies, the common voice of Christians over the centuries remains critically important. The first four Ecumenical Councils of the undivided Church gave expression to this common voice. They are given a special place of honour because at these Councils (held in Nicaea in 325, Constantinople in 381, Ephesus in 431 and Chalcedon in 451) debates about the teaching of Scripture on God, Christ and the Holy Spirit were settled in a way which has been embraced by Christians from all traditions in all generations.[8]

Summaries of 'the faith that was once for all entrusted to the saints' (Jude v3) can be found in a number of places in Scripture (e.g. 1 Corinthians 8:6; 15:1-11; 1 Timothy 3:16). In the early Church, a 'rule of faith' was identified, a core of Christian belief which distinguished orthodox, catholic believers from heretics. Individual beliefs and readings of Scripture could be tested against this foundation. Over time, and with the assistance of the Ecumenical Councils we have mentioned, this rule came to take formal shape in the three historic Creeds – popularly known as the Apostles' Creed,

---

[8] There are some exceptions, for instance the Monophysite churches of the East who have never accepted the Definition of Chalcedon.

the Nicene Creed and the Athanasian Creed.

These Creeds make no attempt to be exhaustive. They do not give an account of everything that Christians believe or everything that is taught in Scripture. What they do provide is a confession of those indispensable truths that lie at the heart of our faith. Each of them has a trinitarian frame. They are confessions of our faith in God the Father, God the Son and God the Holy Spirit. Within this frame, the focus is very clearly on Jesus Christ, the incarnate Son, who is at the centre of God's purposes for the universe. Taken together, these Creeds affirm central biblical truths such as God's creation of all things, his provision of salvation in Christ, the coming judgement of all men and women, heaven and hell, the Christian hope of Jesus' return, and the means which God has provided so that we might live as his faithful people while we await that great day.

The Apostles' and Nicene Creeds have an important role in Anglican liturgy. They provide the congregation with an opportunity to confess before each other and in the presence of our Lord the faith which we all share. The Athanasian Creed has been less commonly used liturgically, but it remains an important reminder of the trinitarian character of our faith. However, these Creeds are not the possession of any one group. They are expressions of the faith of the one, holy, catholic and apostolic Church. For this reason no individual or group is at liberty to change the theology they express. They continue to be authoritative declarations of the Christian faith, and we are bound to acknowledge their relevance and submit to their authority.

The Creeds themselves speak of one holy catholic and apostolic Church. This is sometimes misunderstood. The Church of Christ is *one*. The total fellowship of Christians is Christ's indivisible body. Jesus' final prayer for his Church is for its unity (John 17). The unity of the Church centres around its 'one Lord, one faith, one baptism, one God and Father of all, who is over all and through all and in all' (Ephesians 4:5-6). This Church is *holy*, set apart as the possession of the holy God and bought with the blood of the sinless Christ. The Church, ideally, is a community which is in the world but not of the world, distinct in its faith, morals and the dispensation of these ideals to the world. 'But you are a chosen people, a royal priesthood, a holy nation, a people belonging to God, that you may declare the praises of him who called you out of darkness into his wonderful light' (1 Peter 2:9). The Church is *catholic* in the sense of its common orthodoxy and its mandate to uphold the faith in every time and place. This informs the nature of our Anglican heritage. The Church is *apostolic* because it rests on the foundation of the apostolic witness to Christ. The teaching of the apostles of Christ is the treasure of the Church which shapes its life and witness.

Clause 4: The doctrine of the Church

> *We uphold the Thirty-nine Articles as containing the true doctrine of the Church agreeing with God's word and as authoritative for Anglicans today.*

1.   *The Thirty-nine Articles*

The Thirty-nine Articles of Religion (1571), a slight revision of Thomas Cranmer's Forty-two Articles of 1553, were designed 'for the avoiding of diversities of opinions' and not as a comprehensive statement of Christian doctrine in the manner of some other Reformation 'confessions'. They have long been recognised as the doctrinal standard of Anglicanism, alongside the Book of Common Prayer and the Ordinal.

The Clause should not be interpreted to suggest an equivalence of the authority of the Articles with the authority of the Bible. The authority of the Articles comes from their agreement with the teaching of Scripture. The Articles themselves insist that 'whatsoever is not read therein [i.e. in Scripture], nor may be proved thereby, is not to be required of any man, that it should be believed as an article of the Faith, or be thought requisite or necessary to salvation.' (Article VI). The Articles make no attempt to bind the Christian mind or conscience more tightly than Scripture does on matters of doctrine and Christian living. However, acceptance of their authority is constitutive of Anglican identity.

Historically, assent to the Articles was a prerequisite for ordination throughout the Anglican world. The earliest Anglican canons insist that this assent should be given 'willingly and from the heart'. In recent years, some member churches of the Anglican Communion have dispensed with assent to the Articles, presenting them as mere 'historical documents' or relics of the past. Not coincidentally, these same churches include the ones which have abandoned historic doctrinal and moral standards. For other churches, the Articles have formal authority but they have been neglected as a living formulary. The Jerusalem Declaration calls the Anglican church back to the Articles as being a faithful testimony to the teaching of Scripture, excluding erroneous beliefs and practices and giving a distinctive shape to Anglican Christianity.

Some of the Articles are intended as expressions of central biblical teaching, held in common with other churches of the Reformation. Though they were written in the midst of sixteenth-century debates about Christian doctrine, the Articles remain critically important for the church today. Articles dealing with the nature of God, for example, and with the authority of Scripture and the way of salvation, come into this category. Other Articles, however, are specific to the established English church and must be expressed differently in other contexts. The Articles do not address all the urgent issues of our day, but they do offer first principles and a framework for approaching the Bible which enable us to grapple with new questions and new challenges.

2.   What is the Church?

Our understanding of the Church is grounded in our understanding of the nature and purposes of the triune God. The Church is the people of God (1 Peter 2:9), the body of Christ (1 Corinthians 12:27), the bride of Christ (Revelation 21:9), and the Temple of the Holy Spirit (1 Corinthians 3:16). New Testament teaching regards the Church as having a corporate identity as God's people, called to corporate worship and to corporate mission responsibility to the world.

The Church is God's creation and not simply a human institution, as shown clearly in Ephesians 1:3-14. God has chosen and called his people; Jesus Christ has redeemed his people, and we have been given the Holy Spirit as the promise that God will bring his work to completion. This understanding is echoed in the Ecumenical Creeds.

The Articles focus on the visible church: 'The visible Church of Christ is a congregation of faithful men, in the which the pure Word of God is preached, and the sacraments be duly ministered according to Christ's ordinance in all those things that of necessity are requisite to the same.' (Article XIX). Practically this means that the church exists wherever two or three are gathered around Christ as he is presented to us in word and sacrament. The church is a visible expression and anticipation of what the Bible calls 'the new humanity' which God is creating in Christ (Ephesians 2:15). The church is also an expression of reconciled humanity, a community in which the Holy Spirit dwells (Ephesians 2:19-22). Its goal is the gathering described in Revelation 7:9, 'a great multitude that no-one could count, from every nation, tribe, people and language, standing before the throne and in front of the Lamb.'

The Holy Spirit empowers the church to serve its Lord, Jesus Christ, and equips it to participate in Christ's own mission. The Holy Spirit convicts people of sin, empowers them for service, comforts them and reveals God's truth to them. The particular work of the Holy Spirit can be seen gloriously in the history of revivals, charismatic renewal and mission in many parts of the world. The work of the Holy Spirit in the church does not imply that he is subject to the institution of the church, nor that he is a possession of a particular part of the church. The Holy Spirit is greater than the church, and is at work in the world, directing people to Jesus (John 16:13-15). On more than one occasion the New Testament speaks of the Holy Spirit as the Spirit of Jesus (Acts 16:7; Romans 8:9).

3. The nature of a 'Confessing' Fellowship

The Fellowship has the character of a renewal movement. Like other renewal movements, the Fellowship intends to work within the global Anglican Communion. The Statement makes it clear that the Fellowship 'is not breaking away from the Anglican Communion', and is not claiming to be the sole representative of true Anglicanism.

The Fellowship of Confessing Anglicans is 'confessing' in the sense of confessing the gospel, the faith of Christ crucified. It is confessional in the sense of affirming, as authoritative, the rule of faith found in the historic Creeds and Councils, and in the classic formularies of the Church of England – the Thirty-nine Articles, the Prayer Book and the Ordinal – all of which claim to be in accordance with Scripture, and all of which may be 'proved' by Scripture. The Jerusalem Declaration is itself confessional in form, with brief statements of principle and half of its clauses referring back to existing authorities.

Confessions and other foundational and ecumenical statements must be weighed against the teaching of Scripture. In Jerusalem on 29 June 2008 the Jerusalem Statement was signed by seven Primates and acclaimed by 291 bishops and nearly a thousand clergy and lay people, representing about forty million Anglicans worldwide, who recognised it as faithful expression to the teaching of Scripture. Such a reception and consent, given by the Jerusalem gathering, invests the Declaration with a particular significance as the basis for the governance of the Fellowship. Nevertheless, we must reiterate that the authority of any confession or statement is found in its conformity with the teaching of Scripture.

4. *What do we mean by Anglican?*

As Anglican Christians we proclaim our belief – in the words of the Nicene Creed – in one catholic and apostolic Church, and – in the words of the Apostles' Creed – in the holy catholic Church. We believe that we are part of this Church and, in common with other Christians, we claim antiquity and continuity from the apostles and the Church of the New Testament. The Anglican expression of the gospel is authentic because it is both biblical and catholic. In the words of Article XIX, 'The visible Church of Christ is a congregation of faithful men, in the which the pure Word of God is preached, and the sacraments be duly ministered according to Christ's ordinance'.

As Anglicans we trace our roots through the events of the sixteenth century in England to the earliest Christian witness in Britain, itself a product of the missionary activity of the Roman church. The sixteenth century has a particular significance because this was the period of the Reformation when, in common with what happened in other parts of Europe, the church in England was reformed in the light of Scripture. Archbishop Thomas Cranmer and others did not try to start a new church, but looked to preserve what was helpful in the existing liturgical orders, reforming them in the light of Scripture.

This Anglican church was largely confined to the British Isles until the great missionary movements, beginning in the eighteenth century but flourishing in the following centuries. The twentieth century witnessed the maturing of missionary churches to become Anglican provinces in their own right, thereby forming what is now commonly known as the Anglican Communion. Formal structures emerged to assist what the 1930 Lambeth Conference recognised as a fellowship of self-governing provinces, united by their adherence to biblical principles and Anglican forms of ministry and worship.

5. Anglicans today

The Anglican church is a family within the wider one, holy, catholic and apostolic Church.

We are already *one* because we are each in Christ, united to him in his death and resurrection. God's covenant with us is expressed in the sacraments of baptism and the Lord's Supper. The sacraments of baptism and the Lord's Supper proclaim the gospel of Jesus crucified and risen, and are God's good gift to his people. They call forth and nourish faith and, as covenantal signs, they are an expression of our unity. ('Because there is one loaf, we, who are many, are one body, for we all partake of the one loaf.' 1 Corinthians 10:16-17) Our unity is God's gift rather than our achievement, an answer to Jesus' prayer in John 17. It is in the light of this reality that we are eager to maintain that unity of the Spirit in truth in the bond of peace (Ephesians 4:25 and 4:3), because we belong to the one Lord who prayed that his disciples might be one, and also because we are members of one body (Ephesians 4:25).

We are *holy* (1 Peter 2:9) because we have been sanctified by the blood of Jesus (Hebrews 10:29; 1 Corinthians 1:30) and are now summoned to live as his saints (1 Peter 1:13-16). This is why the church cannot ignore the serious threat to its life as God's people which comes through the embrace of unholy patterns of behaviour (2 Corinthians 5:9-13).

We are *apostolic* because our life together is founded on the faith of the apostles, and we are called, like them, to go into the whole world with the good news of Jesus Christ (Matthew 28:18-20).

We are *catholic* because we acknowledge that we are part of the universal Church stretching through history and throughout the world, and eagerly looking forward to the time when we shall stand before the throne of God and of the Lamb (Revelation 22:3).

Clause 5: The Lordship of Christ

We gladly proclaim and submit to the unique and universal Lordship of Jesus Christ, the Son of God, humanity's only Saviour from sin, judgement and hell, who lived the life we could not live and died the death that we deserve. By his atoning death and glorious resurrection, he secured the redemption of all who come to him in repentance and faith.

This Clause intends to show that, through faith, we accept the unique and universal Lordship of Jesus Christ, and see it also as the centre of the gospel, or Good News, which we believe and which we are commissioned to proclaim. The Apostles subscribed to it and proclaimed it as 'the good news' among their contemporaries. The uniqueness of Jesus and his universal Lordship are attested biblically, in the accounts of his incarnation and the demonstrations of his divine identity, and they are unambiguously confirmed in the creeds, which every confessing Christian upholds as truth and proclaims liturgically during worship (i.e. the Apostles' Creed and the Nicene Creed).

Thus, as we hear these truths we are to respond in submission and loving obedience in lives of worship. Jesus' ministry climaxed in his glorious resurrection and ascension, which validated his claim to be the only bringer of God's kingdom and salvation for all humanity, which will be fulfilled at his return (Acts 2, 1 Corinthians 15). The proclamation of Jesus' Lordship is all the more urgent in the light of contemporary challenges; in some places, inviting people to follow Christ as Lord is claimed to be offensive, and Christians are persecuted.[9]   The acceptance of Jesus' human and divine natures, which together bear witness to his uniqueness and his universal Lordship, is fundamental and basic to the Christian faith; failure to accept it puts one outside the Christian fold, while to discount it as a Christian makes one an apostate (1 John 4:2–3).

1.   The humanity and divinity of Jesus Christ

Jesus, in his incarnation, stands out as distinct and unique – in the following ways:

> Jesus was miraculously conceived and born of a virgin (Luke 1:26-31). His coming was foretold in prophecy and his birth was accompanied by mysterious events (Matthew 1:22-23; 2: 5-6; Luke 2:8-28).

> The Gospel of John presents his spectacular miracles as 'signs' of his divinity (John 20: 30-31). These are often associated with the astonishing claims that Jesus makes about himself in his 'I am' sayings (John 4:26; 6:35; 9:5; 10:7,11; 11:25; 14:6; 15:1).

> All the Gospels report his unique sacrificial death on the cross, his resurrection and ascension. All the Gospels record a voice from heaven endorsing key moments of his life on

---

[9] Persecution happens when the proclamation of the uniqueness of Christ and salvation in him alone is seen as a judgement on other religions and cultures, and as an attack on the integrity of a culture.
This is particularly true in contexts where the poor see and experience salvation in Jesus as the only means of their own liberation. This is the issue of persecution in many parts of India.
In other contexts the choice for Christ is seen as upsetting the existing social arrangements, as is the case among indigenous peoples in Latin America.
Persecution also occurs where biblically faithful Christian proclamation has been lost from the life of the institutional church. In North America an example of this is the virtual expulsion of orthodox congregations from their Anglican provinces, and in South America, gospel preaching has been met with hostile responses from nominally Christian institutions.
Christian proclamation is also resented because it goes against the cultural consensus of pluralism, both in religiously plural cultures and, increasingly, in Western liberal cultures.

earth: at his baptism (Luke 3:21-22), at his transfiguration (Matthew 17:5, Mark 9:7-9), and when he spoke of his death at the time of Passover (John 12:28-30).

The New Testament teaching about Jesus' special relationship with his Father reveals truth which had not been taught before:

> An early Christian hymn, quoted by Paul, says that 'God exalted him to the highest place and gave him the name that is above every name, that at the name of Jesus every knee should bow' (Philippians 2:10).

> An angelic message was given to Joseph that 'he [Jesus] will save his people from their sins' (Matthew 1:21).

> Peter, speaking of Jesus in the power of the Holy Spirit, declared that 'salvation is found in no one else' (Acts 4:12).

> The writer to the Hebrews asserts that Jesus is universal, and that he is for all generations 'the same yesterday and today and for ever' (Hebrews 1:1-4; 13:8).

> The Gospels record the words of Jesus about himself, that the Father has entrusted all judgement to the Son (John 5:22), that he himself has been given 'All authority in heaven and on earth …' (Matthew 28:18), and that the world will be assembled before him for judgement (Matthew 24:30).

2. The response to the Lordship of Jesus Christ

Belief in Jesus' divinity, genuine humanity and universal Lordship gives us the boldness and courage to proclaim him to all mankind. This belief is at the heart of the tradition which the Church receives and submits to, and which she is expected to pass on faithfully from generation to generation. Under no circumstances is the Church in a position to change this reality (1 Corinthians 11:23; 15:3; 1 Thessalonians 4:1; 2 Timothy 2:2).

As God in human form (Philippians 2:9-10), Jesus receives our worship, praise and adoration. Through him, we have access to the Father and have come to know the Father and the Holy Spirit with whom he constitutes the Trinity. We pray through him to the Father (John 15:16; 16:23), and he gives us the Holy Spirit, who guides the Church (John 16:12,13).

42

By reason of Jesus' unique position in the Godhead, and his universal Lordship, we hold his name and person in the highest honour and respect. Faithful Christian men and women experience a high degree of disquiet, when respected church leaders and theologians offend their sensibility and faith, portraying Jesus as other than what the plain reading of Scripture presents him to be. Arguments put forward concerning issues on which the Scriptures are silent do not advance the course of the gospel, nor do they strengthen the faith of the body of Christ. The practice of depicting Jesus in despicable terms undermines the truth of our faith, as well as disparaging the Son of God. Important figures of other faiths attract honour and respect from their devotees! Scripture must be read with a reverent heart, and Jesus, as portrayed in Scripture, must be respected and worshipped, with humility and reverence.

3. The life and death of Jesus Christ

Jesus is the image of the invisible God (Colossians 1:15; 2:9; see also John 1:1,14; Hebrews 1:3). Through his incarnation he reflects the character of God (what God is like), and at the same time displays what it is to be a full and true human being (what man should be like). Jesus was born into our world, shared our nature, and showed us how to live the perfect life that God intends us to live.

In his earthly ministry as a human person, Jesus had human needs and desires: he needed food to sustain his body, power to carry out his plans, and companions to share his life with. Yet in all his human needs he submitted fully to the will and desire of God. When tempted to sacrifice his spiritual mission to the fulfilment of his physical and sensual needs, he resisted by referring to appropriate scriptural texts – 'It is written ... It is written ... It is written ...' (Matthew 4:4,7,10). In doing this Jesus gave us an example of how to obey the word of God and resist the desires and lusts of the flesh. Having triumphed over sin, the world and the devil, he offers help to those who need it, 'For we do not have a high priest who is unable to sympathise with our weaknesses, but we have one who has been tempted in every way, just as we are – yet was without sin. Let us then approach the throne of grace with confidence, so that we may receive mercy and find grace to help us in our time of need' (Hebrews 4:15-16).

Humanity was estranged from God and lost in sin, when God, in love, sent his son to die for the world, because the wages of sin is death (Romans 5:8; 3:23; 6:23). In his body Jesus bore our sins, and his atoning death on the cross won for us our salvation by restoring our fellowship with God. This good news of human redemption and new life in Christ is the Church's message for the whole world. Jesus' earthly ministry is a demonstration of the nature of God, who loves and cares for his creation, and has sent Jesus to save it. Faced with the ministry of Jesus, men and women are challenged to live a life of holiness, reflecting the character of God; such a life will also prepare them for the second coming of Christ (Matthew 5:48). Failure to respond to God's invitation of love, by repenting and putting one's trust in Christ, as the Scriptures exhort us to do, will be met with judgement. The apostles proclaimed this message of impending judgement, along with the good news of new life in Christ (Acts 17:30-31). For those who do respond to God's invitation of love, the suffering and death of Christ ushers people into the embrace of God's grace, and prepares them to stand in Christ's righteousness at the final judgement.

4. Resurrection, ascension and hope

A believer puts his trust in God through repentance and faith, based on what Christ has done. By shedding his blood, Christ has paid the supreme sacrifice for sin and opened the gate of eternal life for believers. The redemptive work of Christ secures for humanity complete freedom from the shackles of sin and the oppressive powers of the present age. Through Christ the believer passes from death into life (John 11:1-45). The all-sufficiency of the atoning work of Christ is proclaimed in the Scriptures, and regularly affirmed in the Eucharistic service, as 'a full, perfect, and sufficient sacrifice, oblation, and satisfaction, for the sins of the whole world' (Book of Common Prayer, the Prayer of Consecration).

The validity of the Christian faith rests upon the saving work of Christ on Calvary, his resurrection and his glorious ascension. The faithful believe this without reservation, because it is in the strength of this that they go out to tell the Christian story of salvation (Matthew 28:19; Acts 1:8; 1 Corinthians 1:23-25). Through our baptism into Christ's death we have died to sin. Sin no longer has any power over us; it has ceased to control us, and we no longer serve it as a master (Romans 6).

Because of Jesus' resurrection, we have the promise and hope of life to come. Having been united with him through our baptism, we rise to a new life. We are alive to God and we now live for his glory. Therefore, we no longer use our bodies for our own purposes or our own gratification. Instead we offer our bodies in God's service, to be used by him as instruments for achieving his righteous purposes (Romans 12:1-2).

With Christ's ascension to the Father, we now worship him as Lord, Master, Saviour, and King. Worship demands love and obedience. To worship Jesus is to love him, obey him and follow him: '*If* you love me, you will keep my commandments' (John 14:15, 21, 23). Such dedication and commitment to Jesus may cause the believer to be misunderstood, persecuted or even martyred.

Clause 6: Anglican heritage

> *We rejoice in our Anglican sacramental and liturgical heritage as an expression of the gospel, and we uphold the 1662 Book of Common Prayer as a true and authoritative standard of worship and prayer, to be translated and locally adapted for each culture.*

1.   *What is our sacramental and liturgical heritage?*

We acknowledge two sacraments given by our Lord Jesus Christ – Baptism and the Lord's Supper (also known as the Holy Communion or Eucharist). These are gospel sacraments, 'effectual signs of grace, and God's good will towards us', and by them faith in Christ is strengthened and confirmed (Article XXV). They are given to invite a response in faith and in order to feed faith in Jesus Christ. They are his gifts, and as stewards we are obliged to be responsible in administering them.   Ministers of the gospel sacraments are called to be careful in their preparation and to teach people to be serious in their reception. Faith in Jesus Christ is absolutely central to the proper reception of the sacraments (Article XXVIII). They are sacraments of the Christian community which direct our attention to what God has done for us in Christ, and are meant for those who acknowledge Jesus as Lord. In this connection we affirm the baptism of infants and look for Christian faith in the parents and the sponsors.

We have a liturgical heritage, and our administration of the sacraments is liturgical. However, we are not free to create liturgical forms according to our personal preferences, or in ways which take us beyond biblical parameters. Our responsibility to the faith entrusted to us, and our responsibility to each other as brothers and sisters in fellowship, rules out unilateral action in this area. Central to our common identity as Anglican Christians is the 1662 Book of Common Prayer.

2. What is the place of the 1662 Book of Common Prayer?

The Jerusalem Declaration affirms the 1662 Book of Common Prayer, while recognising that many parts of the Anglican Communion have other forms of liturgy. Archbishop Thomas Cranmer's liturgical achievement culminated in the Book of Common Prayer of 1552, which was republished with minor alterations and additions in 1662. This has been the standard liturgical resource for Anglicans ever since, translated into many languages and adapted to different circumstances. The orders of service found in this book, together with Cranmer's prefaces, provide an important and distinctive approach to Anglican sacramental and liturgical life.

Several developments over the past century have challenged the traditional place of the 1662 Prayer Book. The modernisations and democratisation of the English language has made the Prayer Book sound quaint or even unintelligible to many contemporary people. Pentecostal forms of worship have attracted many, and Anglican churches in many places have developed informal patterns of corporate worship, with less obvious structure than those found in the Prayer Book. Others have turned to the worship patterns of the early church, and a new liturgical movement has flourished in some parts of the Communion.

These developments have brought many benefits. However, sometimes the changes come with a theological agenda in which the focus on scripture, repentance, forgiveness, thanksgiving and praise is lost or subsumed. In particular some Anglican churches have introduced liturgies which replace the terms for God the Father with functional or 'inclusive' substitutes. The more radical forms of these liturgies are now barely recognisable as Christian.

The 1662 Book of Common Prayer remains a true and authoritative standard of worship and prayer, because the principles it embodies are fundamentally theological and biblical. The liturgies of this book enable all who participate to think in true and biblical ways about God and about their life as his people. The central role of Scripture is reflected in the language of the Prayer Book liturgy, with the result that far more of the word of God is heard in this liturgy than in many other forms of service used by other denominations. Also prominent in the Prayer Book is the lectionary, which is designed to ensure that Scripture is read in a systematic way. The emphases placed on corporate prayer, on the confession of sin and the declaration of God's forgiveness, and on the proper relationship between word and sacrament, remain a check on the dangers of superficiality and self-centredness.

Cranmer's genius lay in preserving those elements of earlier orders of service which communicated gospel truth, and then expressing them in the vernacular language of the day. This resulted in liturgy which not only reflected the existing culture, but also helped to reshape it. His prefaces provide principles for continued liturgical revision, so that in every age gospel truth may be conveyed and celebrated without confusion. Translation and local adaptation are not just contemporary responses to our own needs – they were envisaged in the Book of Common Prayer itself.

We should not expect uniformity of liturgy across the Anglican Communion, but we should look for a common theological basis. Our commitment to the principles underlying the liturgy of the Prayer Book should produce forms of corporate worship which may be diverse, but which still bear a family resemblance. The 1662 Prayer Book provides a standard by which other liturgies may be tested and measured. One key principle of revision is that new liturgies must be seen to be in continuity with the Book of Common Prayer. For example, where 1662 gives *Our Father which art in heaven*, to have *Our Father in heaven* is recognisably in continuity, whereas something like *Our Mother which art in heaven* most certainly is not. This latter phrase is also inconsistent with biblical teaching and Anglican traditions of expression. Another example is the prayer for the English monarch in the Book of Common Prayer; it is recognisably in continuity with the Prayer Book to pray for traditional and political leaders in countries where the Queen has no authority or position.

A second key principle of revision should be that of mutual accountability within the Anglican Communion. The further removed a proposed liturgy may be from the 1662 Prayer Book, the more important it is that it should be subject to widespread evaluation throughout the Communion.

Clause 7: Clerical orders

We recognise that God has called and gifted bishops, priests and deacons in historic succession to equip all the people of God for their ministry in the world. We uphold the classic Anglican Ordinal as an authoritative standard of clerical orders.

1. What do we mean by 'ministry' in the church?

We affirm that Christ himself is the chief minister and source of all ministry within the Church. He is the Shepherd and Overseer of our souls (1 Peter 2:25). He called a people to himself, instituted the sacraments and gave the Church authority and mission, orientation and goal. He exemplified and defined ministry as service in his teaching (Mark 10:45) and by taking a towel to wash the feet of his disciples (John 13:4-5). Christian ministry is not the sole possession, nor the sole responsibility, of those who have been ordained. Ordained ministry is set in the context of the ministry of all believers.

We affirm lay ministry, not only in a clearly ecclesiastical context, such as the ministry of Readers, teachers and evangelists, but also the ministry which takes place in the workplace and in the local community. In fact, ministry is about the service of God that is undertaken in every hour of every day. There is a priesthood of all believers inasmuch as we all have direct access to God through Jesus Christ, and we are all called to witness, to evangelise, and to serve him in all our activities.

It is the task of ordained ministers 'to prepare God's people for works of service, so that the body of Christ may be built up' (Ephesians 4:12). The gifts distributed by the Holy Spirit to each member of the body are to be used 'for the common good' (1 Corinthians 12:7). It is by working together, proclaiming Christ and living as his faithful and loving disciples, that the various orders of ministry function properly.

2. What do we understand about the ordained ministry?

Before and after his resurrection, Jesus Christ provided for the care and nourishment of his Church by giving his word to his apostles (Matthew 28:18-20; John 17:20) and then, on the day of Pentecost, by pouring out his Spirit (John 14:15-17; Acts 2:32-33). From the earliest days of the Christian Church, it has been a vital concern to recognise those whom God has called and gifted to serve and lead his people (Acts 6:1-7; 13:1-3).

The historic threefold order of bishop, priest (or presbyter) and deacon is a particular expression of these New Testament concerns. This order became widespread in the early years of the Christian Church and was retained at the time of the English Reformation; it is still the pattern to which Anglicans are committed, in obedience to Scripture and out of respect for our history.

The Anglican Ordinal (which has been bound within the Book of Common Prayer since 1552) sets out the qualities and responsibilities of each of these orders of ministry, and provides a form of recognition that those so ordained are called and gifted by God. It also reminds all bishops, priests and deacons that those they serve are the precious body of Christ, and that they are responsible to him for the faithful discharge of their ministry.

Bishops are called to be the chief pastor in their diocese, to teach the Christian faith, to banish error, to live a godly life and be gentle with the flock, properly to administer the sacraments, and to lead in mission. Bishops uniquely are to ordain and send out others in ordained ministry.

Priests are called to be 'messengers, watchmen, and stewards of the Lord: to teach and to premonish, to feed and provide for the Lord's family; to seek for Christ's sheep that are dispersed abroad, and for his children who are in the midst of this naughty world, that they may be saved through Christ for ever.' [10]

Deacons are called to serve and assist the Church's ministry.

Each minister is to provide an example of Christian living to other people. And, since ministry is a precious gift, each minister is accountable for it. There is a rightful dignity to the ordained ministry, but this is never merely a human pride. It is the dignity of the cross-bearing servant, faithfully following the master.

Ordained ministers are always and only ministers of the gospel of our Lord Jesus Christ. This gospel is entrusted to them (1 Timothy 1: 12-14), and they are accountable to the Lord for their faithfulness to it. We acknowledge, as part of our Anglican heritage, that no ordained minister is beyond accountability within the body of the church. In extreme cases, where, for example, there are clear breaches of the requirements of the Ordinal, the person concerned, though ordained or consecrated, forfeits the rights and dignity of the office which had been entrusted to that person. Nevertheless, it must be stressed that such a verdict may not be reached quickly, lightly or without considerable prayerful thought and widespread consultation.

Clause 8: Human sexuality

We acknowledge God's creation of humankind as male and female and the unchangeable standard of Christian marriage between one man and one woman as the proper place for sexual intimacy and basis of the family. We repent of our failures to maintain this standard and call for a renewed commitment to lifelong fidelity in marriage and abstinence for those who are not married.

Humanity is created as male and female in the image of God

---

[10] Concerning the nature of the Church, its catholicity and its mandate to uphold the faith in every time and place, see the commentary on Clause 3, final paragraph (p.34).

(Genesis 1:27). This is the biblical understanding of authentic human identity, personhood and value (Genesis 9:5-6). Since maleness and femaleness are gifts of God in creation, they are both part of what it means to be human. Moreover, since male and female are both of equal value, because both share alike in the image of God, equal value exists despite distinctions between the sexes. Gender difference does not mean inequality; equality between men and women, however, does not mean that men and women are interchangeable, so that, for instance, a man can be a wife to another man. Human beings are made to image God to his world and to change the world in obedience to his purpose and will (Genesis 1:26).

The gendered nature of our existence, as male and female, is a critical element in the diversity and yet the unity of the human race. It is to be honoured as God's gift. God has given marriage as the most important expression of unity rejoicing in difference between the two sexes. Jesus reiterates God's original intention for marriage: 'Haven't you read ... that at the beginning the Creator "made them male and female", and said, "For this reason a man will leave his father and mother and be united to his wife, and the two will become one flesh"?' (Matthew 19:4-5). Jesus underlines the fundamental nature of marriage in God's world, and indeed marriage, designed before the Fall, is the sacred institution for society (Genesis 2).

Elsewhere the Bible describes marriage in the richest terms. Not only is heterosexual marriage used by God to explain and illustrate his covenant relationship with his people Israel (Hosea 1 and 2), thereby emphasising his love, faithfulness and care, but also marriage itself is described as a covenant (Malachi 2:14). As such it brings obligations of covenant faithfulness, as well as the joys of mutual human love between a man and a woman (Ephesians 5:21ff, Song of Songs).

Marriage is closely related to procreation, family and children. This is one of the purposes the Bible envisages for it (Malachi 2:15) and it cannot be separated from the creation command to be fruitful and fill the earth (Genesis 1:28). Procreation and the command to multiply relate to a human race that is orientated towards the future, with hope for that future and a sense of responsibility for it, since it implies the coming generations of our descendants. It therefore stands against a view of human existence that sees life in terms of this generation only, such as is to be found in same-sex relationships in which childbirth is an impossibility. Marriage itself is also presented as an institution of real power: it brings a person out of the network of parental relations (in itself a relation of great strength and power) and combines that person with another person in a new relationship, of such unity that it is described as 'one flesh' (Genesis 2:24). Only such a powerful institution as marriage can provide the foundation for human social life; marriage is the basis for the continuation of the human race as God intended.

Malachi 2:15 also stresses that God desires faithful covenantal marriage to be the matrix for nurturing children as godly offspring. In fact, it is well established that a male and a female parent provide the best environment for the raising of children in a more general sense too. The Christian faith has given special emphasis to the care and raising or nurture of children, in whom God's creative activity is renewed. In the incarnation Jesus' experiences included childhood, and in his ministry he made children an example to all who would enter the kingdom of God. Thus marriage and family are critically important for the nurturing of children who represent this aspect of God's love and purpose for his creation.

Being made in the image of God reminds us that our identity and nature is dependent upon him, and derived from him. We are therefore not independent beings, who can 're-make' ourselves as we see fit. This means that we do not have the right or the ability to say of our minds or bodies that they are absolutely ours to do with as we will (Romans 12:1ff). The use of our bodies is not a matter of indifference. It is within the heterosexual marriage relationship that sexual intimacy is appropriate and good. Men and women are encouraged to delight in the sexual dimension of their nature, in the context of an exclusive lifelong relationship between a man and a woman. This stands against contemporary Western culture, in which the main focus is on self and individual fulfilment. In Western culture sex has become immensely important in society, and in addition postmodern culture affirms choice, feelings, the body and aesthetics, placing them above the biblical understanding of sexual morality.

One analyst of Western culture insists that people approach relationships increasingly with the attitude that sexuality is plastic.[II] In other words, priority is given to my feelings that this relationship is authentic and fulfilling for me, and bodily sexualities are subservient to that. The identity of human beings is found in their bodies, but the particularity of gender and sexuality is thought to be a construction. The conclusion, therefore, is that the individual can be sovereign over his or her own sexual choices, and that this must not be determined by outside forces or tradition, for that would be to deny his or her authentic self.

Personhood, on this account, is tied to personal agency (a person's ability to choose for himself or herself and to act to make something happen). This is applied to the freedom that people must have to express their real self in whatever sexual experience they find fulfilling. To constrain a person's agency over his or her own body is the most devastating attack on that person's freedom.

Thus the present-day controversy over sexuality is intimately related to current Western thought, concerning the development and experience of identity, personhood and agency. People with same-sex attractions claim that these experiences define, and are fundamental to, who they are. This is why they are deeply offended when the Church, speaking out of two thousand years of Christian discipleship and biblical teaching, tells them that the very thing they have used to construct their identity is an expression of disobedience to God and his good purposes for human beings. The Church is heard only to be condemnatory, undermining everything that they understand about themselves.

In affirming the teachings from Scripture, the Church must begin by offering a different view of personhood and identity. First, we are made in the image of God (Genesis 1:27), in relationships and as male and female, to act to change the world in obedience to God's purpose and will: to be fruitful, multiply and subdue the earth (Genesis 1:28). These relationships cannot be separated from the way we make use of our bodies. One important use of our bodies is procreation, which requires male and female.

[II] Anthony Giddens.

53

Since this is how God has established human beings in creation, it follows that those accounts of human gender which see it as capable of being *constructed*, either by the individual or by his or her society, are refusals to accept the created and given nature of human identity. Any identity, whether gender-based or otherwise, which is made by human beings for themselves, instead of accepting the identity given by God, is a false identity. It may exercise tragic power, but it is fundamentally false. Similarly, an account of same-sex attraction or promiscuous heterosexual compulsion which alleges that these are God-given impulses – 'This is the way God has made me' – likewise fails to account for the way that these are distortions of God's original intention for heterosexual marriage and relationships, and as such they reflect not God's will but the brokenness of creation.

In spite of the brokenness of creation, which continues to affect our relationships, God acts in reconciliation to reconnect and renew what has been broken. God's redemption addresses our sins and brokenness by making us a new creation. But, sexual relationships that seek to establish relationship in contravention of the connections that God gives for fulfilment continue the brokenness of relationships. Gay liberation tries to find such fulfilling reconnection and fulfilment through connectedness with sexual partners of the same gender, but by ignoring God's creational intention they in fact continue the brokenness of relationships.

The Christian account of personhood is that we are to find our identity as children of the creator God, as redeemed in the second Adam, and invited into the community of the people of God. In that community, its own relationship with its saviour, Jesus Christ, is mirrored in this earthly existence in the covenantal relationship of heterosexual lifelong marriage. Within this community, therefore, marriage is held in high honour. But neither marriage nor sexual activity itself defines a person's identity. Therefore high honour is also to be given to those who, like Jesus, devote their bodies to the service of the Lord and others in singleness (Matthew 19:12; 1 Corinthians 7:32-35).

On this view, therefore, people who claim to find their identity in terms of their same-sex attraction undermine the Christian understanding that identity is a gift of God, which liberates people from the constraints of their history. They also undermine the biblical teaching on the covenant between Christ and the Church, which is his bride, because this cannot be reflected in a same-sex relationship; Christ points to the creation of male and female as the grounding for marriage (Matthew 19:4-6), but a same-sex relationship contravenes this. Here is the biblical and theological basis for the Bible's consistent prohibition on homosexual behaviour (1 Corinthians 6:9-10).

Throughout its history, the Church has understood the lifelong monogamous union of a man and a woman to be God's unchangeable standard (Lambeth 1920, Resolution 66). Most African Anglicans have affirmed monogamy; the prevalence of polygamy among some professing Christians, and also the keeping of concubines, are scandals requiring attention by the Church.

According to Scripture God hates divorce (Malachi 2:16), and Jesus warned that the remarriage of a divorced person is in fact adultery, 'except for marital unfaithfulness' (Matthew 19:9). The main Anglican tradition has permitted divorce but not remarriage, although Archbishop Cranmer seemed open to make exceptions for the innocent party in the case of adultery or abandonment. In recent years, some Anglican churches have opened the floodgates to divorce and remarriage, even among the clergy. The Jerusalem Declaration acknowledges that the Church has failed to uphold and nurture lifelong marriage, and needs to review what conditions justify the remarriage of a divorced person and, in particular, what standards should be required of those in leadership within the Church.

Clause 9: The Great Commission

> *We gladly accept the Great Commission of the risen Lord to make disciples of all nations, to seek those who do not know Christ and to baptise, teach and bring new believers to maturity.*

In all the post-resurrection narratives of the four gospels, the victorious and risen Jesus, who had conquered his foes (Colossians 2.15), charged his disciples to continue his mission of extending the kingdom of God. It is a task that involves 'making disciples'

(Matthew 28:18-20), 'preaching the gospel' (Mark 16:15), proclaiming the message of 'repentance and forgiveness of sins' (Luke 24:47), and participating in God's mission in and through Jesus (John 20:21). The task is to reach 'all nations' and 'all the world'.

This Great Commission is a continuation of the mission of Christ, who came 'to preach good news to the poor ... to proclaim freedom for the prisoners and recovery of sight for the blind, to release the oppressed' (Luke 4:18). Proclaiming Christ involves sharing his concern for the everyday plight of men and women. As Christians proclaim salvation in Jesus alone, love drives them to minister to the whole person – to his or her spiritual, psychological and physical needs. Human rebellion against God not only breaks relationship with God, but also leads to consequences for individuals and society; it alienates people from family, friends and a correct self-image, and deprives them of good health and protection against evil spirits. God does not abandon them, but has sent his Son to bear these consequences by dying on the cross, rising again and bringing a new creation (Ephesians 2:1-10). This is the good news that we, as the Church, continue to proclaim.

This mission is God's mission: *he* has initiated it (Genesis 3:15), *he* has sent Jesus to accomplish it, and *he* will ensure its completion. Through his Spirit, he sends, guides and empowers the Church in this mission. The Holy Spirit convicts a person of his sins (John 16:8), draws him to Jesus Christ, causes him to be 'born again' (John 3:3ff) and enables him to grow in holiness. The Holy Spirit makes the believer a worshipper of Jesus and a witness for him. The Holy Spirit draws the believer into a community, the Church. Though a person can only come to Jesus as an individual, once that person is with Jesus, he or she is never alone. Besides the companionship of Jesus, there is the companionship of other believers, as the new believer becomes a member of Christ's Body, the Church. It is in this community that the Holy Spirit causes all believers to grow into maturity. With unity and love being generated by the Holy Spirit, this body of Christ's disciples becomes a magnet, drawing others towards him (John 13:34, 35; 17:20-23).

This mission can only be done in and through Jesus Christ. It is true, of course, that God displays his being and character through the created order (Genesis 1; Psalm 19; Romans 1), and that men and women of various creeds and none have contributed to our understanding of the created order and human life – some of them testifying to the restless anxiety of those without God. It is also true that God's image in men and women, though marred, is still evident, even in those without faith. Nevertheless, we maintain that a true knowledge of God, and a relationship with him, can only come through Jesus Christ. God himself has not ordained anyone else or any other way by which a person may know him, be forgiven of his or her sins, have a meaningful life with God now, and receive the promise of heaven (John 14:6, Acts 4:12). St Paul, for example, though he made some use of the Greek poets, still proclaimed Jesus, whom God had appointed to 'judge the world with justice' (Acts 17). This is the mission and message of the Church.

Yet this mission is to be done with the utmost 'gentleness and respect, keeping a clear conscience' (1 Peter 3:16). We acknowledge our failure always to respect the dignity, cultures or race of those people with whom we have confidently shared the gospel, and we repent. We have not always demonstrated the goodness, grace and holiness of God. Nevertheless, a life changed by the gospel of Jesus Christ remains one of the most powerful ways of fulfilling the mission committed to the church.

Every Christian is obliged to carry out this mission, in spite of all the political, social and cultural challenges which contest the reign of Christ. It should start with his or her own home and vicinity, but it does not end there. Christ's call is to make disciples of all nations. The controlling vision should be that of 'a great multitude that no-one could count, from every nation, tribe, people and language, standing before the throne and in front of the Lamb', worshipping him (Revelation 7:9).

Clause 10: Stewardship of creation

We are mindful of our responsibility to be good stewards of God's creation, to uphold and advocate justice in society, and to seek relief and empowerment of the poor and needy.

The priority of gospel proclamation does not mean that this is our only responsibility as Anglican Christians. In line with God's intention when placing the first man and woman in the Garden of Eden, we acknowledge our responsibility to be stewards of God's good creation (Genesis 1:28-30; 2:15). The creation itself declares the glory of God (Psalm 19:1). God has revealed his invisible qualities of eternal power and his divine nature through his creation (Romans 1:18 ff). True worship of God involves the recognition that the world and its resources belong to God (1 Chronicles 29:11-24, Psalm 24) rather than to us, and so responsible engagement with our environment should never be isolated from a faithful response to the God who made both it and us. Being good stewards will involve both long-term preservation and the sustainable use of the world's resources.

God has revealed saving knowledge of himself through his Son (John 14:6; John 17:3), who himself spoke of the gospel mission having a special reference to the poor. He came, in fulfilment of Old Testament prophecy, 'to preach good news to the poor' (Luke 4:18). The gospel itself empowers all people, and especially the poor, by giving those who were no people a new identity as sons and daughters of God through repentance and faith in Jesus. This gives to them a future and a hope in God and, in the present, the confidence to address the challenges of their circumstances in the fellowship of a new family, which stands with them as they live as disciples of Christ. As poor people respond to the gospel, its full meaning is unfolded – with empty hands men and women receive grace from God and come to enjoy abundant life (John 10:10). The gospel brings real hope to real people, and so concern for the poor and needy is an integral part of the Church's mission.

In addition, we have a responsibility to love our neighbour as ourselves. This love involves responding to the immediate need of those around us by seeking to remedy it, following the example of the Samaritan in Jesus' parable (Luke 10:25-37). Short-term aid, though, while not unimportant in itself, is not the final solution to poverty and may even become patronising. Systemic and structural problems need to be addressed, and strategies need to be adopted that will enable those caught in a cycle of poverty to escape from it. Love involves respecting and empowering those in need as well as responding to their circumstances.

Our God is a God of justice and he commands his people 'to act justly and to love mercy and to walk humbly with your God'

(Micah 6:8). Throughout the Scriptures God insists on honesty and integrity at all levels of our dealings with each other (Exodus 23:6-7; Proverbs 11:1; 17:15; Micah 6:8). God is also the ruler of the kings of the earth. Christians are called to be loyal citizens of their country. They are also called to be loving critics and critical lovers of their country. Corruption and deceit need to be dealt with appropriately. In mixed societies Christians have a responsibility to demonstrate just dealings in their own lives, and to do all they can to promote justice on the larger scale. The Church must engage with, and prophetically challenge, political and community leaders, in order to bring about change in society that will bring benefit to all (Jeremiah 29:7). Of particular concern will be persecuted minorities, where love and justice call for prayer and protest on their behalf (Galatians 6:10).

Clause 11: Christian unity

> *We are committed to the unity of all those who know and love Christ and to building authentic ecumenical relationships. We recognise the orders and jurisdiction of those Anglicans who uphold orthodox faith and practice, and we encourage them to join us in this declaration.*

On the night before he died, Jesus prayed for the unity of all who believe in him (John 17:20-21). This unity was to be not merely theoretical, but was to show itself in a common love and purpose. Such unity is the work of the Holy Spirit, rather than a human achievement. Nevertheless, Paul would later call on Christians to 'make every effort to keep the unity of the Spirit through the bond of peace', a maturity which he also described as 'unity in the faith and in the knowledge of the Son of God' (Ephesians 4:3,13). Expressing and preserving our unity with all who have come to Christ in faith is an important aspect of our life as his disciples; sadly, we have not always valued this as we should.

We are one in Christ through the Spirit who creates and sustains our unity. Our acts of unity, interceding for one another and partnering one another in mission, flow from the truth that we are united.

This unity requires an honest acknowledgement of our differences, and also a willingness to work at understanding why they exist. Genuine unity can only flourish where there is both humility and a willingness to speak the truth to each other in love. Authentic ecumenical relationships cannot be built on ambiguity or a reluctance to engage in difficult conversations. These relationships do not require agreement on every point, in order to be authentic, but they do call for a serious respect for those who share a commitment to obey the teaching of Scripture, but with whom we may continue to disagree on some matters.

Anglicans who uphold orthodox faith and practice, though they may differ on various matters and come from various traditions – Evangelical, Anglo-Catholic, Charismatic – recognise in each other genuine brothers and sisters in Christ; they will also recognise properly ordered ministry. We offer each other support and encouragement, and provide pastoral care and oversight in places where, for whatever reason, it is not available. This Jerusalem Declaration is itself an offer of fellowship and encouragement, held out to all who share in our commitment to preserve and promote the faith once for all delivered to the saints, an offer held out equally to those in the Anglican Communion who do not at present feel prepared to identify with this Fellowship. It is a matter of great sadness that, following the events of 2003 in The Episcopal Church in the USA, 'broken communion' between Anglicans has become a global reality. Our hope and prayer is that God will bring repentance and reconciliation so that fellowship and communion may be restored.

Clause 12: Freedom and diversity

We celebrate the God-given diversity among us which enriches our global fellowship, and we acknowledge freedom in secondary matters. We pledge to work together to seek the mind of Christ on issues that divide us.

1. *What do we understand about diversity in the Church?*

Our understanding of the Church is grounded in the doctrine of

God as Trinity. Three Persons in one Godhead provides us with a model of diversity in unity and unity in diversity, such that unity and diversity can never finally be separated. The relations between the Persons of the Trinity are those of equality of Being and a mutual indwelling of love. Yet the divine Persons are not identical, and the eternal relations are ordered, not symmetrical. This understanding of God helps us to see that, within the Church, unity does not mean uniformity; there can be legitimate diversity.[12]

The diversity we see in creation, in the plant and animal worlds, is remarkable and sometimes breathtaking – a wonderful reason to praise the Creator. The diversity in human culture, as it has developed around the world and still continues to evolve in new and complex forms, is also vast. This diversity is more apparent than ever before, with the speed and extent of communication in our modern world. But we cannot assume that all of it is in accord with the purpose of God, who sets principles for human diversity in the Scriptures, to enable us to discern its limits.

As a global fellowship, we celebrate our diversity of culture, style, tradition and churchmanship as being God's wonderful gift to us. We are excited about the possibilities it brings for us to learn from each other, strengthen our commitment to a common mission, and see our individual cultural preferences in a wider perspective. We understand that this will require a continued generosity towards each other, and also a willingness to uphold a legitimate diversity of opinion and practice under the canopy of biblical truth.

It has to be admitted, however, that not all attitudes towards diversity can be affirmed. Because of the Fall, some attitudes can lead to division. For instance, differences of ethnicity may be part of the richness of our world, but when these are handled with human pride and self-assertiveness the result may be oppression and even violence.

When we come to think about diversity of lifestyle and social practice, we recognise that not all forms of this diversity are morally

---

[12] Concerning the Trinity and the nature of the Church, see the commentary on Clause 4, under the heading 'What is the Church?' (p.36)

legitimate. Some are clearly contrary to the teaching of Scripture. Article XX of the Thirty-nine Articles defines the limits of the Church's freedom in this matter, stating that 'it is not lawful for the Church to ordain any thing that is contrary to God's Word written'.

Article XX also asserts the principle that Scripture does not contradict itself: '... neither may [the Church] so expound one place of Scripture, that it be repugnant to another.' Such a prohibition implies that all Scripture is internally consistent, because it is all God's word, and God is not inconsistent; it would be wrong, therefore, to suppose that Scripture *might* contain contradictions. This principle gives additional value to the Article, in that it allows us to accept diversity in matters that are *not* 'repugnant' to Scripture. It helps us distinguish between primary and secondary matters.

2. What are primary and secondary matters?

In principle this is an easy question to answer. Primary matters are those directly addressed by Scripture and which call for our faith and obedience. The transgression of such matters would call for repentance, and so diversity cannot permitted here. One example is the teaching in Scripture that Jesus is the way, the truth and the life (John 14:6). Such teaching banishes the idea that Jesus is simply the only way for Christians, or that he is one way among various other options. This is a primary matter.

Another example is the scriptural teaching that homosexual practice is offensive because it is contrary to the creation purposes of God. Scripture's denunciation of this behaviour is consistent throughout the Old and New Testaments. On this basis it is equally a primary matter that no practising homosexual person should receive holy orders or, if already ordained, continue in those orders.

Secondary matters fall into two categories: those on which Scripture teaches freedom and those on which Scripture is silent. In the first category is Paul's teaching about diet (Romans 14:13-23). Paul sees the content of the diet as a matter of individual freedom. But there is a primary matter here also, in that no Christian is free wilfully to offend another in the name of freedom. In the second category come music, forms of corporate worship, dress and so on. Scripture gives no categorical commands on these matters, and here we need to respect and guard the freedom in Christ that we have been given.

However, the question is not always straightforward, particularly at points where Christians disagree as to whether a matter is primary or secondary. Sometimes we may have to live in unremitting love with unresolved tension, determined to think and pray together but accepting legitimate differences, and looking forward to the day when we will have a common mind.

3. What is the way ahead over issues that divide us?

We recognise that we who are united in making the Jerusalem Declaration still disagree over some important issues. In such cases we are committed to working together, praying and studying the Scriptures together, in confidence that God is able to teach, reprove, correct and train us through his word (2 Timothy 3:16-17), bringing us not simply to a consensus but to the mind of Christ (1 Corinthians 2:16; Philippians 3:15). We are also committed to maintaining the proportions of Scripture, in the way that Article VI suggests, when it distinguishes between those things contained in Scripture which are 'necessary to salvation', and those which are 'not read therein, nor may be proved thereby'.

We do not think this will be easy. Conversations may be lengthy. Our various viewpoints are held conscientiously and many have long been a part of our traditions. Our own sinfulness (especially our pride) may get in the way. Nevertheless, we will not give up on the possibility of coming together in submission to the word of God, to pursue 'unity in the faith and in the knowledge of the Son of God' (Ephesians 4:13).

Clause 13: Orthodox faith and false teaching

> *We reject the authority of those churches and leaders who have denied the orthodox faith in word or deed. We pray for them and call on them to repent and return to the Lord.*

It is a matter of deep grief to us that some churches and leaders, who have been charged with the responsibility of teaching and living the truth, have denied the orthodox faith and the clear moral instruction of Scripture by their words and by their deeds (cf Matthew 5:19). With dismay, many orthodox Christians have heard bishops deny the uniqueness of Christ, the necessity of repentance and faith for salvation, the abiding authority and relevance of the Scriptures, and the goodness of God's pattern for relationship between sexes, particularly in the area of sexual intimacy and family life. These denials have brought harm to those who make them, to those entrusted to their care, and to all of us. They have hampered our mission to the world, causing scandal in the eyes of those who reject Christ and attack his Church.

1. *By what authority do we break communion with those who deny the orthodox faith?*

The word of God in Scripture is itself a 'double-edged sword' which judges our hearts and God's Church (Hebrews 4:12; Revelation 2:16). Those propagating the different gospel have rejected biblical authority and the Church's historic rule of faith, and thus they have already forfeited their authority. They have chosen to walk apart, authorising things that are contrary to Scripture. But the Church does not have the right or the power to prescribe anything that is contrary to Holy Scripture (Article XX). It is on the basis of this prior spiritual authority of Scripture that the churches making up this Fellowship derive their authority to break communion. Indeed, there is a moral obligation to reject any teaching that denies or undermines the authority of God as revealed in the Scriptures, to expose its falsity and to break fellowship with those who promote it (Ephesians 5:11; Titus 3:10).

2. *Who are we to reject the authority of false teachers and teachings?*

Clause 13 is speaking on behalf of the whole assembly gathered in Jerusalem in June 2008. The same assembly that acclaimed the Jerusalem Declaration urged the Primates' Council to declare that they are in full communion with confessing Anglican jurisdictions, clergy and congregations, and thus to authenticate them, and conversely to withdraw recognition from others who have denied the faith. Any decision to reject an official but false ecclesiastical authority can only be taken collectively at the highest level. In the case of this Fellowship, this means that it can only be made by the Primates' Council, at present, or a wider synod of bishops in the future.

3. *Who are the recipients of this rejection?*

The Fellowship of Confessing Anglicans recognises, sadly, that there are already bishops, dioceses and whole provinces within the Anglican Communion which promote a different gospel. It should be emphasized that this rejection is not meant to extend to the many faithful clergy and laypeople in heterodox jurisdictions. We pray that they may be comforted in their hearts, enlightened in their minds, and strengthened for witness to the truth.

The Bible gives guidelines for the disciplining of false teachers, and these guidelines include calls for repentance and, finally, separation (1 Corinthians 5:1-5; 1 Timothy 1:20). While there is no exact precedent within the Anglican Communion for dealing with the present situation, historically, orthodox bishops and churches have declared themselves to be out of communion with heterodox leaders and bodies, following councils such as Nicaea and Chalcedon. We acknowledge that the breaking of communion between churches is to be applied only in extreme circumstances, such as those which led to the Conference in Jerusalem in 2008. Church discipline should be exercised with due process and over time. In 2001, two Primates presented to the Primates' Meeting a proposal entitled 'To Mend the Net'.[13] Although the Primates at that time failed to take up this proposal, we commend the following as a pattern of discipline:

1. *Self Examination.*[14] Jesus' warning to 'judge not lest you be

---

[13] *To Mend the Net: Anglican Faith and Order for Renewed Mission* (ed. Drexel W. Gomez and Maurice W. Sinclair; Carrollton, Tx.: Ekklesia Society, 2001), pp.9-23.

[14] Side-headings are taken from *To Mend the Net*, with an addition to point 7. Exposition is taken from Stephen Noll, *The Future of the Anglican Covenant in the Light of the Global Anglican Future Conference* (January 2009): http://www.stephenswitness.com/2009/01/future-of-anglican-communion-covenant.html. There is a fuller discussion of *To Mend the Net* in 'The Decline and Fall (and Rising Again) of the Anglican Communion', an address given to the Mere Anglicanism Conference on 16 January 2009: http://www.stephenswitness.com/2009/01/decline-and-fall-and-rising-again-of.html.

judged' is a gospel truth: people are often ready to cast the speck from their neighbour's eye while ignoring the log in their own (Matthew 7:1-5). This is the reason for St Paul's exhortation: 'Examine yourselves to see whether you are in the faith' (2 Corinthians 13:5). In the weighty matter of breaking communion, leaders must be particularly vigilant as to their own hearts.

2. *Educative Role.*   Heresy is rooted in deceptive, worldly understandings (Colossians 2:8). Hence it is important that leaders, when separating themselves from such understandings, should give an orthodox 'reason for the hope that [they] have' (1 Peter 3:15).

3. *Advanced Sharing.*   Any decision to break communion should involve patient consultation among orthodox leaders to establish the reasons that such separation is necessary.

4. *Preparation of Guidelines.* Leaders should work according to established guidelines and not act arbitrarily in a crisis mentality.

5. *Godly Admonition.* Admonition is out of favour in today's morally permissive and doctrinally indifferent climate, yet it is still essential to church leadership (1 Thessalonians 5:12). So orthodox leaders must give clear warning and time for repentance to those who have gone astray.

6. *Observer Status.* Paul urges the Corinthians to deliver the sinner to Satan 'so that ... his spirit [may be] saved on the day of the Lord' (1 Corinthians 5:5). Applying this to a church context, those provinces or bishops who violate the orthodox faith should, after due warning, be excluded from joint activities and structures, in order that they may repent before it is too late.

7. *Continued Evangelism [and Pastoral Oversight].* This step justifies 'interventions' in jurisdictions that are, in effect, on probation. Observer status (see point 6) creates a vacuum of proclamation of the gospel, both for those who have heard a false gospel and for those who have never heard the gospel, and pastoral care for those who believe is disrupted. During such a period of probation, the work of the Church must go

on, even if it is opposed by those being disciplined.

8. *New Jurisdiction.* There comes a time in the disciplinary process when it is acknowledged that those who have offended will not repent, that they have hardened their hearts to the gospel (Hebrews 4:4-6). The process of discipline, therefore, may require the formation of an alternative jurisdiction, under new leadership.

According to the Global Anglican Future Statement, the sequence of steps leading to step 8 has already occurred, in relation to The Episcopal Church (USA) and the Anglican Church of Canada, and on that basis the Primates' Council has encouraged the formation of a province in North America, to uphold orthodox faith and practice. This being so, we want it to be understood that the action of breaking communion is intended to take evangelism and a prophetic voice to the needy world, as well as protecting the Church from error.

We recognise that some Anglicans have been deceived by false teaching, and we pray that they may be enlightened and may return to sound fellowship. Finally, we pray for those false shepherds who have misled others, praying that they may come to see their error, repent, and receive the grace of Christ's forgiveness.

Clause 14: The return of Christ

We rejoice at the prospect of Jesus' coming again in glory, and while we await this final event of history, we praise him for the way he builds up his Church through his Spirit by miraculously changing lives.

When Jesus ascended into heaven, those who witnessed this great event were told that he would 'come back in the same way you have seen him go into heaven.' (Acts 1:11). This reflected Jesus' own teaching while he was with them. He had told them that he would 'come back' (John 14:3) and that his return would be 'in his Father's glory with his angels' (Matthew 16:27). It is no wonder, then, that the apostle Paul could describe Christians as those who have 'turned to God from idols to serve the living and true God, and to wait for his Son from heaven' (1 Thessalonians 1:9-10). Confident anticipation of the return of Jesus has been the centrepiece of Christian hope since the very beginning.

We look forward to his return. The event will be both joyful and fearful. Joyful because we shall see Jesus 'as he is' (1 John 3:2). To meet with someone whom we have worshipped, loved and served all our lives is an occasion to look forward to. We yearn to rest from our labours, to have all our doubts cleared or rendered irrelevant, to realise that those efforts performed in his name have not been in vain, to realise that the sufferings for his sake have been all worthwhile, and to hear his voice say, 'Well done, good and faithful servant! ... Come and share your master's happiness!' (Matthew 25:21).

Yet it is also a fearful event. Christ shall return to 'judge the living and the dead' (2 Timothy 4:1). There will be those who are rewarded and there will be those who are shut out from the presence of the Lord, 'the second death' (Revelation 21:8). This judgement has already begun with 'the family of God', the Church (1 Peter 4:17). Commentators agree that the judgement of God does not spare the Church; if judgement begins with the Church, by purifying it through persecution, how much more severe will it be on the rest of society. Christ foretold that his disciples would be persecuted by the nations, or be deceived by false prophets. Some who followed him would turn away from the faith, while the love of others would grow cold (Matthew 24:9-13). St Paul too spoke of these 'last days' and warned Timothy to have 'nothing to do' with those who have 'a form of godliness but [deny] its power' (2 Timothy 3:5). The judgement of God on the world and the Church has already begun.

In the meantime, we have not been left alone. The ascended Christ has poured out his Spirit on the Church (Acts 2:14-21) and continues to build his Church, both in number and in maturity. He continues to work miraculously as the gospel is preached to the ends of the earth (John 14:12; 1 Corinthians 12:28). He transforms lives as he brings men and women to new birth, puts his Spirit within them, and builds them into his own likeness (John 3:5; 2 Corinthians 3:18).

This is more than the transformation of individuals, however. Christ continues to be at work in the Church. The prospect of Christ's return prompts us to holy living (2 Peter 3:11-13) and faithfulness in service (1 Corinthians 3:12-15). He is preparing the Church for that day when he will 'present her to himself as a radiant church, without stain or wrinkle or any other blemish, but holy and blameless' (Ephesians 5:27). He is preparing a 'bride beautifully dressed for her husband' (Revelation 21:2). That husband is Jesus Christ himself, who says, 'Behold, I am coming soon!' (Revelation 22:7)

And when he comes, he will inaugurate the new heaven and the new earth, in which God's reign of justice and peace will be established for all, 'The kingdom of the world [will] become the kingdom of our Lord and his Christ' (Revelation 11:15), he will hand over the kingdom to his God and Father, and God will be all in all (1 Corinthians 15:24, 28). This is an inspiration for the hearts of believers for deep joy, confidence in the final victory of God, perseverance in the face of opposition, and strength to endure suffering and rejection. Even so, come, Lord Jesus!

The Way, the Truth and the Life

Theological Resources for a Pilgrimage to a Global Anglican Future

First published in Israel May 2008

Preface

The Most Revd Nicholas D. Okoh
Archbishop of Bendel, Nigeria
Chairman, GAFCON Theological Resource Group

The decision to write this handbook, to serve as a theological introduction and definition for GAFCON, was reached on the same day, 14 December 2007, in Nairobi, that the leadership team resolved to organize GAFCON. The opening section, *A most agonizing journey towards Lambeth 2008*, explains how, in recent years, huge amounts of time, energy and money have been expended, in the search for an agreeable solution to the human sexuality controversy in the Anglican Communion. It has remained elusive.

In the course of time, it became clear that the issue at stake was much wider than the human sexuality issue concerning same-sex unions. What had been 'in the works' for some years – the challenge to the authority of the Bible, in all matters of faith and practice, both within the Church and in personal morality – suddenly became a public reality when, in 2003, Gene Robinson, a practising homosexual, was consecrated bishop in the United States of America. Later, in 2006, The Council of Anglican Provinces in Africa (CAPA) produced a positional paper, *The Road to Lambeth*, which identified a crisis of doctrine and also of leadership, observing correctly that the Anglican Communion was at a crossroads; it had to decide, without further hesitation, which way to go. One road, that of compromising biblical truth, would lead to destruction and disunity. The other road might have its own obstacles, but it would lead to God and to life. It is this second road that has brought us to GAFCON.

What beliefs do GAFCON Anglicans hold? These papers, written by members of the GAFCON Theological Resource Group, reaffirm our Christian faith as it relates to some prime topics: Anglican identity and orthodoxy, the Lordship of Jesus Christ and its implications for personal morality and in mission, and the whole issue of authority, Christ's authority in the Church and the authority of the Bible. One paper discusses the all-important issue of worship, yesterday, today and tomorrow. These and a few other subjects are briefly addressed in this collection of papers, which is a GAFCON theological handbook.

It must be admitted that the result is imperfect, for several reasons, chief of which is the time constraint. Unfortunately it was not possible to cover further aspects of theology in the time available. The book is being released in advance of GAFCON 2008, as part of our preparation for the conference. Later on it is hoped that a post-GAFCON revision, incorporating fuller discussion and more topics, will be compiled.

It is not the intention of these papers to initiate a fresh debate. We should remember how the church in North Africa and Asia Minor almost totally disappeared, at a time when Christological debate was raging in the church. Instead, the book is offered with the purpose of guiding and educating everyone who comes to GAFCON: bishops and their wives, clergy, and concerned lay people, including young people. So, we hope it will be found to be jargon-free and readable.

The Revd Canon Dr Chris Sugden, our Secretary, has worked very hard from the outset. We owe a huge debt of gratitude to him, and also to our Convener, Dr Vinay Samuel. As members of the Theological Resource Group, we have enjoyed a wonderful bond of brotherhood in the Lord, during the preparation of this handbook. And we have developed confidence in one another, which I think holds great promise for the future. As a team, we reflect the catholicity of GAFCON, having come from Kenya, Uganda, Nigeria, UK, USA, Australia and India. Here I would like to express, on behalf of the leadership team, our gratitude to our publishers, The Latimer Trust, for their readiness to work with us. Finally, all of us in the Theological Resource Group are immensely grateful to the leadership team of GAFCON for the privilege of this assignment.

A Most Agonizing Journey towards Lambeth 2008

The Most Revd Peter Akinola
Archbishop of Abuja and Primate of all Nigeria

I therefore, a prisoner for the Lord, beg you to lead a life worthy of the calling to which you have been called, with all humility and gentleness, with patience, bearing with one another in love, making every effort to maintain the unity of the Spirit in the bond of peace. (Eph. 4:1-3)

We have been on this journey for ten long years. It has been costly and debilitating for all concerned, as demonstrated most recently by the tepid response to the invitations to the proposed Lambeth Conference 2008. At a time when we should be able to gather together and celebrate remarkable stories of growth, and the many wonderful ways in which our God has been at work in our beloved Communion, with lives being transformed, new churches being built and new dioceses established, there is little enthusiasm even to meet.

There are continual cries for patience, listening and understanding. And yet the record shows that those who hold to the 'faith once and for all delivered to the saints' have shown remarkable forbearance, while their pleas have been ignored, their leaders have been demonized, and their advocates marginalized. At the Lambeth Conference in 1998 we made a deliberate, prayerful decision with regard to matters of Human Sexuality. This decision was supported by an overwhelming majority of the bishops of the Communion. It reflected traditional teaching, interpreted with pastoral sensitivity. And yet it has been ignored, and those who uphold it have been derided for their stubbornness. However, we have continued to meet and pray and struggle to find ways to maintain the unity of the Spirit in the bond of peace.

The journey started in February 1997 in Kuala Lumpur. It was here, during the 2nd Encounter of the Global South Anglican

Communion, that a statement was issued expressing concern about the apparent setting aside of biblical teaching by some provinces and dioceses. The statement pleaded for dialogue in 'a spirit of true unity' before any part of the Communion embarked on radical changes to church discipline and moral teaching.

Sadly, this plea, as with several similar warnings, has been ignored. Ten years later, in February 2007, the Primates of the Anglican Communion met in Dar es Salaam, Tanzania, and experienced an agonizing time as they tried to repair the Communion that had been so badly broken. Their earlier prediction, at the Primates' Meeting at Lambeth Palace in 2003, that rejection of the faith committed to us would 'tear the fabric of our Communion at its deepest level', has proved to be accurate. In Dar es Salaam the Primates proposed, as one last attempt to restore unity, that there should be a period of seven months, during which those who had brought our Communion to the brink of destruction should reconsider their actions, and put a stop to the harmful actions that have so polarized our beloved church.

The Primates set a deadline, 30 September 2007, for receiving an answer. This deadline was ignored.

There is no longer any hope, therefore, for a unified Communion. The intransigence of those who reject biblical authority continues to obstruct our mission, and it now seems that the Communion is being forced to choose between following their innovations or continuing on the path that the Church has followed since the time of the Apostles. We have made enormous efforts since 1997 in seeking to avoid this crisis, but without success. Now we confront a moment of decision. If we fail to act, we risk leading millions of people away from the faith revealed in the Holy Scriptures and also, even more seriously, we face the real possibility of denying our Saviour, the Lord Jesus Christ.

The leadership of The Episcopal Church USA (ECUSA) and the Anglican Church of Canada (ACoC) seem to have concluded that the Bible is no longer authoritative in many areas of human experience, especially those of salvation and sexuality. They claim to have 'progressed' beyond the clear teaching of the Scriptures, and they have not hidden their intention of leading others to these same conclusions. They have even boasted that they are years ahead of others in fully understanding the truth of the Holy Scriptures and the nature of God's love.

Both ECUSA and ACoC have been given several opportunities to consult, discuss and prayerfully respond, through their recognised structures. By way of response they have produced carefully nuanced, deliberately ambiguous statements, but their actions have betrayed these statements. Their intention is clear; they have chosen to walk away from the biblically-based path we once all walked together. And the unrelenting persecution, of those among them who remain faithful, shows how they have used these past few years to isolate and destroy any and all opposition.

We now confront the seriousness of their actions, as the time for the Lambeth Conference draws near. Sadly, this Conference has not been designed, as in the past, as an opportunity for serious theological engagement and heartfelt reconciliation. We are told that it will be a time of prayer, fellowship and communion. These are commendable activities, but this very Communion has already been broken by the actions of the American and Canadian churches. The consequence is most serious, for if even a single province chooses not to attend, the Lambeth Conference effectively ceases to be an Instrument of Unity. Moreover, the status of the Archbishop of Canterbury, as convenor and as an instrument or focus of unity, also becomes highly questionable.

Repentance and reversal by these North American provinces may yet save our Communion. Failure to recognise the gravity of this moment will have a devastating impact.

1. *Scorned opportunities*

Following the 1997 warning, the 1998 Lambeth Conference issued Resolution 1.10. This affirmed the teaching of the Holy Scriptures with regard to faithfulness in marriage between a man and a woman in lifelong union, and declared that homosexual practice was incompatible with biblical teaching. Then, in March 2000, at their meeting in Oporto, Portugal, the Primates reaffirmed the supremacy of Scripture as the 'decisive authority in the life of our Communion'.

However, in July 2000 the General Convention of the Episcopal Church USA responded by approving Resolution D039, which acknowledged relationships other than marriage 'in the Body of Christ and in this Church', and stated that those 'who disagree with the traditional teaching of the Church on human sexuality, will act in contradiction to that position'!

The Convention only narrowly avoided directing the Standing Commission on Liturgy and Music to begin preparation of official rites for the blessing of 'these relationships ... other than marriage'.

In 2001, the Primates' Meeting in Kanuga, North Carolina, issued a pastoral letter acknowledging estrangement in the Church, due to changes in theology and practice regarding human sexuality, and calling on all provinces of the Communion to avoid actions that might damage the 'credibility of mission in the world'. In April 2002, after their meeting at Canterbury, the Primates issued a further pastoral letter, recognising the responsibility of all bishops to articulate the fundamentals of faith and maintain Christian truth.

In what appeared to be an act of deliberate defiance, the Diocese of New Westminster in Canada voted, in June 2002, to approve the blessing of same-sex unions, with the enthusiastic support of their bishop, Michael Ingham. Later that year the twelfth meeting of the Anglican Consultative Council took place in October, in Hong Kong, and a resolution [34] was approved that urged dioceses and bishops to refrain from unilateral actions and policies that would strain communion.

The following year, however, when ECUSA met in General Convention in Minneapolis in July/August, they chose, among their many actions, to reject a Resolution [B001] that affirmed the authority of Scripture and other basic elements of Christian faith. They also approved the election as bishop [C045] of someone living in an unashamedly sexual relationship outside marriage.

The Primates' Meeting specially convened at Lambeth Palace, in October 2003, issued a pastoral statement condemning ECUSA's decisions at General Convention, describing them as actions that 'threaten the unity of our own Communion as well as our relationships with other parts of Christ's Church, our mission and witness, and our relations with other faiths, in a world already confused in areas of sexuality, morality and theology and polarized Christian opinion.' They also declared that if the consecration proceeded 'the future of the Communion itself will be put in jeopardy', and that the action would 'tear the fabric of our communion at its deepest level, and may lead to further division on this and further issues as provinces have to decide in consequence whether they can remain in communion with provinces that choose not to break communion with the Episcopal Church (USA)'. They also called on 'the provinces concerned to make adequate provision for Episcopal oversight of dissenting minorities within their own area of pastoral care in consultation with the Archbishop of Canterbury on behalf of the Primates'. ECUSA responded, the following month, by proceeding with the consecration of Gene Robinson, thereby tearing the fabric of our Communion and forcing the Church of Nigeria, along with many other provinces, to sever communion with ECUSA.

Earlier, in June 2003, we in the Church of Nigeria had cut our links with the diocese of New Westminster, and sent a clear warning about the reconsidering of our relationship with ECUSA, should Gene Robinson be consecrated. As always, we were ignored.

During 2004 there was a growing number of so-called 'blessings' of same-sex unions by American and Canadian priests, even though The Windsor Report, released in September 2004, reaffirmed Lambeth Resolution 1.10, and also the authority of Scripture as being central to Anglican Common Life. The Windsor Report also called for two moratoria, one on public rites of same-sex blessing, and the other on the election to the episcopate, and consent, of any candidate who was living in a same-sex union.

One consequence of this continuing intransigence by ECUSA was the alienation of thousands of faithful Anglicans who make their home in the USA. The attempts by the Primates to provide for their protection, through the Panel of Reference, proved fruitless. So, the desire of these faithful Anglicans for an alternative spiritual home led to many impassioned requests to the Church of Nigeria, and also to a number of other provinces within the Global South. The Standing Committee of the Church of Nigeria recognised this urgent need during their meeting in Ilesa in March 2004 and, as a result, initiated a process for the provision of pastoral care through the formation of a Convocation within the USA.

The Province of Nigeria made the conscious decision to

initiate the Convocation of Anglicans in North America (CANA) in the light of the following:

- the undisputed alienation among Anglicans in North America created by the actions of ECUSA, despite warnings from the Instruments of Communion.

- the need for pastoral care and oversight for alienated Anglicans in North America in the light of the Primates Communiqué in October 2003. 'The provinces concerned to make adequate provision for episcopal oversight of dissenting minorities within their own area of pastoral care in consultation with the Archbishop of Canterbury on behalf of the Primates.'

- ECUSA's establishment of churches in the diocese of Europe.

- The consecration and appointment of Bishop Sandy Millar as a bishop of the Province of Uganda, called to serve in the United Kingdom.

As a matter of courtesy, the Archbishop of Canterbury was duly informed of our intentions.

During the African Anglican Bishops Conference (AABC), in October 2004, the Primates who were present released a statement which, among other things, urged the Episcopal Church USA and the Anglican Church of Canada to take seriously the need for 'repentance, forgiveness and reconciliation enjoined on all Christians by Christ'. It called on these two churches to move beyond informal expressions of regret for the effect of their actions, and to have a genuine change of heart and mind.

Although, at their meeting in The Dromantine, Northern Ireland in February 2005, the Primates advised the withdrawal of both ECUSA and the ACoC from the Anglican Consultative Council, the continued influence of these churches on the Communion, and their renewed efforts to cause others to adopt their intransigent line, frustrated any genuine attempts at reconciliation. The agonizing journey towards unity and faith seemed unending.

The obvious reluctance of the Archbishop of Canterbury, and the unwillingness of the other Instruments of Unity, to effect discipline on those who had rejected the mind of the Communion, prompted the Church of Nigeria to effect a change in her constitution, during a General Synod held in Onitsha in September 2005. This constitutional change not only protects the Church of Nigeria from being led into error by any church in the Communion, but also makes full constitutional provision for the Convocation of Anglicans in North America (CANA).

The Third Anglican South-to-South Encounter, meeting in Egypt in October 2005, issued a very strong indictment of ECUSA and the ACoC, and called for a common 'Anglican Covenant' among churches remaining true to biblical Christianity and historic Anglicanism.

Despite all the calls for repentance, the blessing of homosexual unions, and the nominating of practising homosexuals to the episcopacy, continued in the USA, with the Archbishop of Canterbury expressing 'deep unease' with such nominations in California in February 2006. (An article describing the reaction of the Archbishop of Canterbury, Archbishop Rowan Williams, to the California election is to be found in the Church of England Newspaper, February 24th, 2006.)

The much-awaited ECUSA General Convention in 2006 proved to be a disappointment: resolutions expressing regret for the harm done to the communion were rejected, as was one that tried to emphasize the necessity of Christ for salvation. Among the resolutions that were approved was one promoting homosexual relationships, and another that apologized to homosexuals for the following of biblical principles by the Anglican Communion. A pledge to include openly homosexual persons was requested 'of our sister churches in the Anglican Communion and Anglican Communion bodies as evidence of the apology'. Finally, someone who does not regard homosexual behaviour as a sin, and who does not consider Jesus to be the only way to the Father, was elected as Presiding Bishop. The agony of a frustrated Communion was visible worldwide, except among those already prepared to embrace this dangerous path of departing from the faith.

The Church of Nigeria needed no further prodding to proceed with the election, in June 2006, and then in August 2006 the consecration, of the Rt Revd Martyn Minns, to give Episcopal oversight to CANA. The Nigerian House of Bishops also declared a reluctance to participate in the 2008 Lambeth Conference with an unrepentant ECUSA and Anglican Church of Canada. (The Minutes of the Church of Nigeria's House of Bishops' meeting, in June 2006, confirm this.)

The Global South Anglican Primates, meeting in Kigali in September 2006, recognised that ECUSA appeared to have no intention of changing direction and once again embracing the 'faith once delivered'. In their communiqué they wrote: 'We are convinced that the time has now come to take initial steps towards the formation of what will be recognised as a separate ecclesiastical structure of the Anglican Communion in the USA ... We believe that we would be failing in our apostolic witness if we do not make this provision for those who hold firmly to a commitment to historic Anglican faith.'

The Anglican Communion Primates, meeting in Dar es Salaam in February 2007, reaffirmed the 1998 Lambeth Resolution 1:10 and called on ECUSA (now renamed The Episcopal Church, TEC) to consider definite actions, which could heal the Communion as well as reassure those who had been deprived of adequate pastoral care. The Primates had set a deadline of 30 September, by which date they hoped to have a response. By June 2007, both the ACoC and TEC had indicated an unwillingness to comply with these requests, but had expressed a desire to remain part of the Communion they had hurt so much. The Primates' deadline came, and went; it was ignored. The situation had been made even more incoherent by the decision, made earlier in the year, to extend an invitation to the Lambeth Conference to those responsible for this crisis, with no accompanying call to repentance, but not to invite certain bishops, such as Bishop Martyn Minns, who have stood firm for the Faith. And so, now, we fail to see how these two positions can ever be reconciled.

2.   All journeys must end some day

Therefore, since we are surrounded by such a great cloud of witnesses, let us throw off everything that hinders and the sin that so easily entangles, and let us run with perseverance the race marked out for us. (Hebrews 12:1)

These past ten years of distraction have been agonizing, and the cost has been enormous. The time and financial resources spent on endless meetings, whose statements and warnings have been consistently ignored, represent a tragic loss of resources that should have been used otherwise. It now appears, however, that the journey is coming to an end, and the moment of decision is almost upon us. But this is not a time to lose heart or fail to maintain vigilance. It would be an even greater tragedy if, while trying to bring others back to the godly path, we should ourselves miss the way or lose the race.

- We want unity, but not at the cost of relegating Christ to the position of another 'wise teacher' who can be obeyed or disobeyed.

- We earnestly desire the healing of our beloved Communion, but not at the cost of re-writing the Bible to accommodate the latest cultural trend.

As stated in *The Road to Lambeth*: 'We Anglicans stand at a crossroads. One road, the road of compromise of biblical truth, leads to destruction and disunity. The other road has its own obstacles [faithfulness is never an easy way] because it requires changes in the way the Communion has been governed and it challenges [all] our churches to live up to and into their full maturity in Christ.'[15]

The first road, the one that follows the current path of The Episcopal Church USA and the Anglican Church of Canada, is one that we simply cannot take: the cost is too high. We must not sacrifice eternal truth for mere appeasement, and we must not turn away from the source of life and love for the sake of a temporary truce.

The other road is the only one that we can embrace. It is not an easy road because it demands obedience and faithfulness from each one of us. It requires an unequivocal acceptance of, and commitment to:

- the authority and supremacy of Scripture

---

[15] http://www.globalsouthanglican.org/index.php/comments/the_road_to_lambeth_presented_at_capa.

- the doctrine of the Trinity

- the person, work and resurrection of Jesus the Christ

- the acknowledgement of Jesus as divine, and the one and only means of salvation

- the biblical teaching on sin, forgiveness, reconciliation, and transformation by the Holy Spirit through Christ

- the sanctity of marriage

- teaching about morality that is rooted and grounded in biblical revelation

- apostolic ministry

These are not onerous burdens or tiresome restrictions, but rather they are God's gift, designed to set us free from the bondage of sin and give us the assurance of life eternal.

It is our hope and fervent prayer that, in the coming months, all those in leadership will be directed towards the restoration of true unity in the Body of Christ, by means of an unconditional embrace of the One who says to all who will listen, 'If you love me, you will obey what I command.'

John Bunyan, the author of *The Pilgrim's Progress*, describes the Christian life as a journey from the City of Destruction to the Celestial City. On his journey, numerous decisions and many crossroads confront Christian, the pilgrim. The easy road was never the right road. In the same way, we have arrived at a crossroads; it is, for us, the moment of truth.

This day I call heaven and earth as witnesses against you that I have set before you life and death, blessings and curses. Now choose life, so that you and your children may live and that you may love the LORD your God, listen to his voice, and hold fast to him. (Deuteronomy 30:19,20a)

Authentic Anglicanism

And Jesus came and said to them, 'All authority in heaven and on earth has been given to me. Go therefore and make disciples of all nations, baptizing them in the name of the Father and of the Son and of the Holy Spirit, teaching them to observe all that I have commanded you. And behold, I am with you always, to the end of the age.' (Matthew 28:18-20)

'The times of ignorance God overlooked, but now he commands all people everywhere to repent, because he has fixed a day on which he will judge the world in righteousness by a man whom he has appointed; and of this he has given assurance to all by raising him from the dead.' (Acts 17:30-31)

The all-encompassing Lordship of Christ, the certainty that God's purposes will be fulfilled, and the urgency of Christian mission in the last days – these are the foundational elements which provide both the context and the content of our future as Anglican Christians. This future calls for a renewed determination, on our part, to submit all our thoughts, actions and plans to the scrutiny of God's word, with humble and repentant hearts.

We rejoice in the grace and mercy of the living God, in our identity as disciples of his Christ, and in the heritage of authentic Anglicanism that we have received from those faithful men and women who have gone before us. We rejoice in the presence of God among his people today as, through his word and by his Spirit, he enables us to live before him, and in the world, as men and women being conformed to the likeness of Christ, and committed to proclaiming the salvation that he has won for all who come to him in faith.

Authentic Anglicanism is a particular expression of Christian corporate life which seeks to honour the Lord Jesus Christ by nurturing faith, and also encouraging obedience to the teaching of God's written word, meaning the canonical Scriptures of the Old and New Testaments. It embraces the Thirty-nine Articles of Religion (published in the year 1571) and the Book of Common

Prayer (the two versions of 1552 and 1662), both texts being read according to their plain and historical sense, and being accepted as faithful expressions of the teaching of Scripture, which provides the standard for Anglican theology and practice.

While authentic Anglicanism makes no claim to be perfect, and respects Christians of other traditions, it nevertheless insists on certain basic theological commitments. These are to be found in the classic documents of the Anglican tradition, but they need to be reiterated and reaffirmed in each generation. The non-negotiable core of these commitments includes:

- the goodness, love and mercy of the living God who eternally exists in three Persons, Father, Son and Holy Spirit;

- the creation of men and women by God in his image, with all that this means for the dignity and value of every human life;

- the distortion of creation, at all levels, by the decision of the first man and woman to turn aside from trust in God's goodness, expressed in the word he had given them;

- the lostness of the human race, as the result of the fall into sin, which manifests itself in our natural guilt, corruption and enslavement to sinful desire;

- the uniqueness of Jesus Christ as the incarnate Son of God, and as the only Saviour for sinful men and women;

- the central saving reality of judgement being borne in our place by Jesus Christ on the cross, which is his great victory over all that stands against us, and that also stands opposed to the rightful rule of God;

- the historical actuality and theological indispensability of the bodily resurrection of Jesus Christ from the dead, on the third day after his crucifixion, leaving empty the tomb in which he had been laid;

- the necessity of the Spirit's work in bringing about repentance and faith in the human heart, so as to unite us to Christ and enable us to share in the salvation he has won;

- the right standing with God which is given freely, and which now belongs to all who, by faith, are united to Jesus Christ in his death and resurrection;

- the expectation of the bodily return of Jesus Christ, to bring God's purposes of salvation and judgement to their consummation;

- the significance of the Church as the gathering of the redeemed people of God around the word of God and in the Spirit of God;

- the supreme authority of the Scriptures as the word of God written, and as the source of true teaching about God, his purposes, and the appropriate response to God's mercy in Jesus Christ;

- the purpose of Christian ministry within the churches to nourish faith and obedience through careful teaching of the Bible in the context of genuine personal relationships;

- the generous provision of the Lord's Supper and baptism which, as sacraments, visibly represent the promises of the gospel of Jesus Christ to his people;

- the legitimate exercise of authority within the churches which is characterized by unreserved obedience to the teaching of Scripture and Jesus Christ's own pattern of service;

- the importance of fellowship between Christian congregations in the common cause of living as disciples of Jesus Christ and as his ambassadors in the world;

- the priority of evangelism for all Christians in response to the great commission of Jesus Christ.

What is at stake?

The Anglican Communion has been proud of its comprehensiveness. In recent times, however, some parts of the Communion have been allowed to develop in such a way that their expressions of faith and life, now, can hardly be recognised as being Christian, let alone being Anglican. There are five areas in which we perceive that what has been entrusted to the Church is currently under threat. They are areas, therefore, that are being fiercely contested.

1.   *The struggle over authority, for the Church and for the Christian*

Your word is a lamp to my feet and a light to my path. (Psalm 119:105)

1.1.   The nature of divine revelation, and the nature of the text of the Bible – these are the prime matters being disputed.

All Anglicans agree, formally, that the Bible has supreme authority. But what is the nature of this authority? Is the authority tied to the biblical text, or does it operate independently of it? Or is this authority expressed through a variety of texts, persons and institutions?

We begin with the possibility of our recognising and receiving God's revelation, in spite of our fallen nature. The Fall adversely affected, but has not destroyed, human ability to recognise and receive God's revelation. For God created us for fellowship with himself. Also, importantly, God himself links the revelation with the text through his Holy Spirit, who 'breathes' the text.

1.2.   All Anglicans agree that ultimate authority lies in God alone. The question is, how does he exercise his authority? And how are we to understand the way he acts? Are we to say that he acts in the same way as, and alongside, other actors and agents?

God's authority is not abstract. It is expressed through human persons and institutions, including the family, the Church and the community of the chosen people. Since God links his authority to his words, as given in Scripture, the biblical text possesses a privileged status, in relation to human persons and institutions, precisely because it contains God's words, given and brought home to the human heart by the living activity of his Holy Spirit.

1.3.   How should we understand revelation? It is the presence of God, and it is also God speaking to his people. These two understandings are completely compatible; they are only falsely opposed to one another. God exercises his authority through his Spirit, by means of the words which he addresses to particular human beings. Those who disagree with this claim will ask whether that speech is episodic and time-bound, as would be suggested by its expression in a historical text, or whether it is of a different order from human-to-human speech. It cannot be correct, however, that God's words might be time-bound, for if that were the case the incarnation would be marginalised. The highest expression of divine speech is the Word made flesh, who was with God from the beginning, and who upholds all things by his word of power. In addition, the New Testament writers recognise the Scriptures as being God's speech to us now – the writer to the Hebrews, for example, stresses this in chapters three and four of his epistle. They do not view the Scriptures as a reduced form of communication, or an echo of a word spoken in the past, or as merely a background against which we hope to discern what God is saying to us today.

To take the Bible seriously is to take seriously the one who communicated its words. It should not be supposed, however, that recognising the Bible as God's speech is idolatry. We realise, and acknowledge, that we are under the authority of the Bible, and we expect the word to confront us with new and even strange things. We do not become masters of the word. And God does not reinforce our prejudices!

We are not free to pick and choose in Scripture. All of it is God's revelation, and all of it needs to be taken seriously.

2.   *The struggle over the interpretation of Scripture*

The above view of authority carries with it several implications for the interpretation of Scripture.

2.1.   While some say that the meaning of Scripture is so complex, and so contested, that it cannot be fixed, we argue that the heart of Scripture is plain, even though some parts are not simple. It is plain enough to call forth our faith and obedience, which together lead us to further understanding of the Bible's meaning. It is plain enough to be the basis on which we make a stand.

2.2.   Another element in this struggle is the distinction that is sometimes made between the main teachings of the Bible and the lesser ones, those that are referred to as *adiaphora*, meaning 'things that are indifferent'. According to this view, some doctrinal and moral issues may be put aside because they do not really matter, while others must be affirmed by all. This distinction is seen as essential for the unity of the Church, and yet the Bible itself never applies it in this way. And in Anglican tradition *adiaphora* are primarily matters to do with ceremonies and robes, and not issues concerning doctrine or morality.

2.3.   How are Christians to ensure that their understanding, or interpretation, of Scripture is valid? The historic pattern is that the Church arrives at one mind after meeting together, and deliberating, in Council. It takes care to establish that its decisions are faithful to the teaching of Scripture, and that they stand in continuity with the Church's life and message through the centuries. The Church also seeks to make provision for Christians to test these decisions against the Scriptures, according to the example of the Berean Christians who 'examined the Scriptures daily' (Acts 17:10-12). This is the true meaning of the technical term 'reception'. In the current climate, however, there is often a tension between those who seek a deeper understanding of what has already been given, in Scripture, for example the meaning of God's provision of marriage and family, and those who claim that they have received a new revelation, for example that same-sex activity is holy.

3.   The struggle over theological pluralism in the Church

3.1.   The Anglican Church has always been a confessional institution, but its confession does not seek to be comprehensive on every issue, or to foreclose discussion. Over the last two hundred years, however, an unwillingness has grown up, in some parts of the Church, to bind itself to confessional formulae, such as the Thirty-nine Articles. Instead, there has been a strong move towards a more general affirmation of the Thirty-nine Articles, accepting them as a historical background which informs our life and witness, but not as a test of faith. As long as this unwillingness remains, there is little hope for an effective Covenant within the Anglican Communion.

3.2.   Liberal Anglican leaders and theologians insist, in their rhetoric, upon the comprehensiveness of the Church, but in reality they have problems with a comprehensiveness that includes the orthodox. Comprehensiveness, hitherto, has been maintained by a liberal consensus in which liberals defined the space, setting its boundaries, and provided legitimacy for every section of the Church. This has now broken down.[16] The liberal consensus turned from transcendent realities, about which there was religious dispute, to the reality of the world, which all could supposedly agree on. But this reality is seen to be riven with discord, and in that discord liberals have now taken the side of the victim, and no longer claim universal representation. Since, therefore, liberals in places of power have now insisted on entrenching their views and excluding those who disagree, conservatives are unwilling to be confined to the marginal space assigned to them, and realise that they do not need the liberal establishment for legitimacy.

3.3.   The liberals focus on shared worship, shared work and shared experience, but not on shared faith. In contrast, the New Testament concept of fellowship is anchored in a common faith and a common mind (Philippians 2:1-2; 1 John 1:1-3).

---

[16] See Professor Oliver O'Donovan's sermons: http://www.fulcrum-anglican.org.uk /news/2006/200607030donovan1.cfm?doc=122.

4. The struggle over the understanding of mission

4.1. The Anglican church is committed to proclaiming the gospel of Jesus Christ crucified and risen. For some, however, the church is itself the message. By this they mean that the Anglican church's own diversity, and its ability to live with plurality and contradiction in its own membership on matters of faith, is precisely the witness it gives to a plural society today.

But the Bible teaches that the Church Christ founded is entrusted with a message, and that its members are to be transformed by this message. Paul's teaching, on the relativising of different identities, and on their restoration in Christ, is clear. In the Church of Christ different identities (of race, nationality, class, gender) are not merely included, they are transformed. And they are relativised by being included in the identity of the crucified and risen Lord. They then bear one message: the good news of Christ's death and resurrection, and his transforming power. Christians do not simply belong to a message, they bear that message in their lives.

4.2. Anglican mission has always taken seriously the culture of the diverse peoples in which the gospel is expressed and lived out. At the same time, it has always seen the gospel message as being translatable into any culture, without any fear that its universality might be compromised. This is at the heart of the Anglican Reformation. So, at any time or in any place, the church is both catholic, belonging to the universal church, and part of a particular culture. But because of the givenness of Scripture and the catholicity of the faith, and because the church is the bearer of a transcendent and transforming gospel, it has always been called to confront human cultures, rather than adapt itself to them. A recent example of this was when the church in Kenya confronted the political rulers, whose traditional expectations were to maintain their own dominance through unjust means, with the clear teaching of the Scriptures.

4.3. The contemporary tendency to disconnect belief from behaviour affects the Anglican church today very significantly. The secular view is that behaviour is primarily a personal matter; it cannot be imposed. This means that the belief on which a person bases his or her behaviour is also a personal matter. But biblical teaching calls for behaviour which is compatible with the teaching of Scripture.

Human sinfulness and selfishness easily find rationalisations for chosen behaviours, even behaviours that are clearly contrary to the plain teaching of Scripture. In our day the privatisation of belief, and the perceived need for the expression of individual authenticity, mean that any imposition of behaviour from outside will be rejected. There is no room, however, for such views in a biblically faithful Christian church.

4.4. Contemporary cultures increasingly place Eros, human love, at the centre of human authenticity and fulfilment. It is here that orthodox Christians need to struggle to recover a biblical understanding of human love, as being both profoundly natural and transcendent. In biblical teaching, human love, if it is to be meaningful, satisfying and transcendent, must be expressed in the order that God has provided, in a faithful, monogamous heterosexual relationship. Every other expression, particularly of sexual love, is seen in Scripture as destructive, both of the family, the order that God gives for human flourishing, and of the individual's own wellbeing. For this reason it is forbidden.

4.5. The writings of the Bible emerged in contexts of religious plurality. But the challenge to the people of God was to share the uniqueness of their God in such a context. This challenge still stands, in a world of increasing religious pluralism.

5. *The struggle over post-colonial power relationships*

The issue of Anglican identity is affected by these matters:

5.1. The question of legitimation: Who defines Anglicanism? Who legitimizes the brand?

5.2. Geography: Globalisation has made geographical boundaries irrelevant in most areas of life. People's attachments and identities are no longer primarily geographical. It is this that must now shape the way in which fellowship and accountability are experienced in the Anglican Communion.

5.3. Power and post-colonial realities: The Anglican Communion has yet to face up to the reality of post-colonial Anglicanism, not just in terms of national churches in the non-Western world, but in terms of churches with increasing numbers, and the power that attends such growth. There is an analogy with the rise of China and

India in the global economic world. The rest of the world seeks to adjust and relate effectively to such realities. In Anglicanism, however, the rise is resisted vigorously by some sections, while others embrace it uncritically. The Church, as the first Global Community, is called to demonstrate a way of dealing with power and accountability that witnesses to the transforming power of the risen Lord.

In conclusion – the struggle today is to affirm that the plain truth is accessible to the ordinary person. Those who deny that this is possible then define everything in terms of power, in a situation in which they hold the upper hand and their power is being challenged by this very appeal to truth. Repeated attempts at dialogue have been made by those committed to the teaching of Scripture. However, experience has shown that the revisionists are not willing to listen.

We now turn to examine four issues in greater detail:

> *1. the nature of Anglican orthodoxy, and thus the nature of Anglican identity;*
>
> *2. the implications of the confession that Jesus is Lord, in the Church and in mission;*
>
> *3. how the authority of Jesus is to be expressed and obeyed, and*
>
> *4. how we are to worship God.*

Finally, we look forward to our journey into the future.

1. Anglican orthodoxy

1.1 Anglican orthodoxy defined

The phrase 'Anglican orthodoxy' may sound strange to some ears. Anglicanism, despite many contacts with the Eastern Orthodox churches, has never been in communion with them, nor pretended to be Orthodox in the way that they are. Of course 'orthodoxy' is no more the exclusive domain of the Eastern churches than 'catholicity' is of Rome. Nevertheless, the current use of the term among conservative Anglicans calls for some explanation.

In its basic sense, orthodoxy means 'holding correct doctrine' or, to use a phrase from the East African Revival, 'walking in the light', as opposed to 'walking in darkness' (1 John 1:6-7), which is 'heresy'. The concern for Christian orthodoxy goes back to the time of the apostles. In the later epistles, the theme of sound doctrine being attacked by false teaching is particularly apparent.

- St Paul describes the responsibility of a bishop in this way: 'He must hold firm to the doctrine (*didache*) of the faithful word, so that he may be able to expound sound doctrine (*didaskalia*) and confute those who contradict it' (Titus 1:9).

- For St John, holding true teaching will include a person in the love of God, but holding false teaching will exclude a person from his love: 'Any one who goes ahead and does not abide in the doctrine of Christ does not have God; he who abides in the doctrine has both the Father and the Son' (2 John 9). Indeed, the division between orthodoxy and heresy has serious communal implications, as seen in John's command which follows: 'If any one comes to you and does not bring this doctrine, do not receive him into the house or give him any greeting' (2 John 10).

- Similarly, St Jude, the Lord's brother, writes to the Church, 'appealing to you to contend for the faith which was once for all delivered to the saints' (Jude 3). Jude makes it clear that the particular heresy plaguing the Church has to do with moral teachings from 'ungodly persons who pervert the grace of our God into licentiousness and deny our only Master and Lord, Jesus Christ' (verse 4).

95

From this apostolic teaching the 'rule of faith', or 'rule of truth', was derived. It was on the basis of this that the early Church opposed various heresies, such as Marcionism, Gnosticism and Arianism. The rule was elaborated by the early Councils, whose decisions became creedal for later generations of catholic and orthodox Christians.

Although the Reformation of the sixteenth century burst forth with a new vitality and new learning in many areas, its fundamental claim was that it represented a continuation of, and indeed a return to, the original apostolic faith. Anglican apologists like Bishop John Jewell argued that 'the catholic fathers and bishops made no doubt but that our religion might be proved out of the Holy Scriptures. Neither were they ever so hardy to take any for an heretic whose error they could not evidently and apparently reprove by the self-same Scriptures' (*Apology*, pp.19-20).

One of the Thirty-nine Articles of Religion notes that the churches of Jerusalem, Alexandria, Antioch and Rome have erred in matters of faith, morals and ceremonies (Article XIX). This implies that 'orthodoxy' cannot be equated with any one church or tradition. Instead, it must be proved by Holy Scripture (Article VI). Though the Articles focused on what Scripture reveals concerning those things necessary for salvation, their author, Archbishop Thomas Cranmer, intended that they should also be confessional. Clergy in the Church of England were expected to affirm them 'from the heart' (*ex animo*), and some churches today (e.g. Nigeria) continue this practice. This standard of orthodoxy is upheld by the Anglican Ordinal, in which two key vows are required of priests and bishops: 'Are you persuaded that the holy Scriptures contain sufficiently all doctrine required of necessity for eternal salvation through faith in Jesus Christ?', and 'Will you be ready, with all faithful diligence, to banish and drive away all erroneous and strange doctrines contrary to God's Word ...?'

The universal acceptance of the Prayer Book and the Articles, as standards of Anglican teaching, seemed to guarantee biblical orthodoxy, but, like the church in Ephesus (Revelation 2:1-7), Anglicanism suffered from latitudinarian indifference rather than overt heresy. The regulatory force of the Articles was weakened, from the late seventeenth century, and replaced with a rationalistic moralism. By the mid-nineteenth century, concerns began to arise that the Church of England was no longer ruled by the plain sense of Scripture and its classic formularies. One challenge came from John Henry Newman and the Tractarians, who reinterpreted the Articles in a Roman direction. From the liberal side, Bishop Colenso of Natal was seen to employ 'higher criticism' of the Bible in order to question the authority of Scripture. This latter challenge led to the calling of the first Lambeth Conference. The Lambeth Quadrilateral, adopted at the third Conference, functioned as a means of steering a middle course through the modernist-catholic debates, while promoting a basis for ecumenical dialogue. Some have seen the Quadrilateral as an adequate definition of Anglican orthodoxy, but the current crisis has shown that, without the recovery across the Communion of the classic doctrinal and liturgical formularies, it is inadequate to the task.

The growing strength of liberalism, however, undermined hopes for a renewed orthodox consensus. In particular, English and American Anglicanism fell victim to certain bishops – John A.T. Robinson and David Jenkins on one side of the Atlantic, and James Pike and John Spong on the other – who questioned the very 'substance' of orthodox Christianity: the transcendence of God, the possibility of miracles, the Virgin Birth and Bodily Resurrection of Christ and, underlying all, the authority of the Bible. These bishops kept their office and were, at most, lightly rapped over the knuckles for their controversial views. In the case of The Episcopal Church USA (TEC), such 'prophetic' views were stamped as mainstream with the election of Katharine Jefferts Schori as Presiding Bishop in 2006. Increasingly, the words 'Anglicanism' and 'crisis' began appearing in the same sentence.

At the very time that Western Anglicanism was drifting from the orthodox faith, new movements of Anglicanism were arising in the so-called Global South. Rooted in the nineteenth-century Evangelical and Anglo-Catholic missions, African, Asian and South American Anglicanism became indigenous, part of a wider movement which Philip Jenkins has labelled, rather dramatically, *The Next Christendom*. The Anglican Church of Nigeria, for instance, took Lambeth 1988's 'Decade of Evangelism' to heart, and planted churches that increased its membership from 14 million people to 18 million. (This growth has continued into a second decade, so that Nigerian Anglicans now number about 20 million.)

Anglicans in the Global South were at first surprised, and then appalled, to learn of the promotion of homosexuality by the churches in the West. While some of their abhorrence may be rooted in their culture, much of it derives from their reverence for Scripture. 'The missionaries brought us this book,' one African bishop said at Lambeth in 1998, 'and we are not going to turn our backs on it.' Some of these Anglicans see themselves in a spiritual battle: 'the acts of God versus the acts of Satan', as one Nigerian theologian put it. These Anglicans have now forged alliances with orthodox Anglicans in Western churches such as TEC, the Anglican Church of Canada and the Church of England itself. Though they may be divided as to how to respond to the weak leadership of the Anglican Communion since 1998, the Global South churches are united in their commitment to biblical authority and Anglican orthodoxy.

Whether spelled out by the 2008 Lambeth Conference, in terms of an Anglican Covenant, or evidenced by the convening of the Global Anglican Future Conference (GAFCON), it is clear that there is a need to explore and define anew, for Anglicans worldwide, what it means to be orthodox, and also how they should respond to those who transgress into the territory of heresy.

1.2 Anglican orthodoxy in a global context today

The Articles of Religion, in distinguishing the biblical essentials of salvation from those other matters which may be affected by time and culture, open up the possibility of a significant diversity in orthodox Anglican piety and polity. The typology of three streams of Anglican faith and practice – evangelical, catholic and charismatic – has been widely observed for more than thirty years, especially since the advent of charismatic movements inside the church. Such a typology is easily caricatured and easily misunderstood, like the image of Anglicanism as a three-legged stool (Scripture, tradition and reason). But there is legitimate value in the three-streams model, especially when they are seen as flowing together into one river – no doubt with different currents and eddies. The value of this typology is also enhanced when it is removed from the historical polemics in the Western churches and applied to the Global South churches and the wider mission field.

1.2.1 *Evangelical*

Anglican orthodoxy is, first and foremost, *evangelical.* The gospel of salvation through Jesus Christ – preached, believed and defended, is at the heart of the apostolic message.   Evangelical Christianity is necessarily triune in shape: John Stott defines evangelical priorities as 'the revealing initiative of God the Father, the redeeming work of God the Son and the transforming ministry of God the Holy Spirit' (*Evangelical Truth*, p.25).

The gospel is conveyed through God's word written in Scripture, and preached by pastors from the pulpit and evangelists on the street corner. In the words of the famous hymn,

> The church from her dear Master
> Received the gift divine,
> And still the light she lifteth
> O'er all the earth to shine.
> It is the golden casket
> Where gems of truth are stored;
> It is the heav'n-drawn picture
> Of Christ, the living Word.[17]

Though Islam claims to possess the final word from God, this word may only be read in Arabic. By contrast, Anglican missionaries laboured to translate the Bible and the Prayer Book into the vernacular, and converts were known as 'readers'. Historically, the church has taken the lead in promoting formal education, in all parts of the world, and even today has been involved in founding new universities in East Africa.

The gospel is worth fighting for and dying for.   The preaching of the gospel and its defence in the face of paganism and heresy are God-ordained activities, for all Christians at all times. At the time of the Reformation, Martin Luther's cry – 'Here I stand, I can do no other!' – epitomized the stance of the primitive church. And over the centuries the noble army of martyrs, those known and unknown individuals 'whose voice cries out', has included countless Anglicans, from the martyrs of Oxford and Uganda to the many in

---

[17] 'O Word of God Incarnate' by William W. How, 1823-1897.

modern times who have lost their lives in Islamic regions.

Besides its emphasis on the gospel, Evangelical Anglicanism has another side: a spirit of liberality. It may seem strange to include 'liberality' alongside *sola scriptura*, the gifts of the Spirit and the cost of discipleship, but it should not be. As St Paul says, '...where the Spirit is, there is liberty.' (2 Corinthians 3:17), and his own pastoral practice as an apostle exemplifies the aphorism: 'In essentials, unity; in non-essentials, liberty; in all things, charity.' Liberality of spirit characterizes the Anglican *via media* approach to doctrinal, liturgical and pastoral matters, which seeks to be firm in matters of salvation and modest with regard to secondary or 'indifferent' matters (*adiaphora*). Going back to John Jewell and Richard Hooker, this 'sweet reasonableness' (Titus 3:2) has been a hallmark of Anglican writers, with George Herbert, C. S. Lewis and John Stott being prime examples.

Though it may be a virtue in secondary matters, tolerance can and does lead to an opposite vice: spiritual laxity, which manifests itself in pastoral laziness and doctrinal slovenliness. In *The Great Divorce,* C. S. Lewis was quick to point out the perversion of liberality, in his portrait of an Anglican bishop who says, 'There is no such thing as a final answer ... to travel hopefully is better than to arrive.' Such smug mediocrity, evident today in the Anglican Communion's turmoil, has led some African church leaders to invoke Tertullian: 'What has Athens to do with Jerusalem, the Academy with the Temple?' They are calling for an unwavering adherence to the Anglican formularies, and also for a rejection of Lambeth's dithering and failure to enforce discipline upon those who have spurned the faith.

1.2.2 *Catholic*

Secondly, Anglican orthodoxy is *catholic,* in the sense that it is universal, applicable to all mankind. It can be no other if it is to be faithful to our Lord Jesus' prayer, 'that they all may be one, Father, just as You are in me and I am in You' (John 17:21). It must also be guided by St Paul's vision of the Church as 'one body and one Spirit – just as you were called to one hope when you were called – one Lord, one faith, one baptism, one God and Father of all, who is over all and through all and in all' (Ephesians 4:4-6).

Anglican orthodoxy is catholic in that it values the catholic Creeds and the Ecumenical Councils of the early church, recognising that these have provided a 'rule of faith' that is derived from Scripture. While honouring the Creeds, Anglican orthodoxy also upholds the substance of the Protestant confessions, recognising that they contain key insights into the truth of the gospel. In particular, it offers the Articles of Religion as an abiding contribution to the wider Christian church, and claims them as normative for its members.

Anglican orthodoxy agrees with the historic traditions that 'praying shapes believing', and that liturgies are of great importance, both in communicating the faith and in sustaining Christian disciples. In particular, it sees the classic Book of Common Prayer (1662), and its authentic translations and modernizations, as expressing the substance of the faith in the context of worship. As with the Articles, it sees the Prayer Book as constituting a lasting contribution to the wider Christian church. Anglican orthodoxy incorporates a variety of ceremonials and styles of worship. It upholds the importance of the sacraments of baptism and Holy Communion as 'effectual signs of grace'. And it values the office and role of bishops in maintaining the faith across space and time.

In response to Christ's Great Commission, the scope of Anglican orthodoxy is worldwide, embracing 'every nation, tribe, people and language' (Revelation 7:9). By God's providence, the Anglican Communion is represented in every region of the world, by Christians from the different races, ethnic groups and cultures which emerged from the heritage of the British Empire, who now belong to indigenous and autonomous churches. Anglican orthodoxy is also ecumenical in spirit. It is eager to participate in ecumenical dialogues and partnerships, with Roman Catholics and the Orthodox, and with various Protestant bodies, e.g. through the Lausanne movement.

It is this very desire, to maintain the true unity of the Body, that has led many orthodox Anglicans to unite together, in the face of the false Christianity that has sprung up within the Communion. The current crisis for Anglican orthodoxy is, in fact, part of a wider crisis among the historic churches of the West. As J.I. Packer puts it:

Time was when Western Christendom's deepest division was between relatively homogeneous Protestant churches and a relatively homogeneous Church of Rome. Today, however, the deepest and most hurtful division is between theological conservatives ("conservationists" I would rather call them), who honor the Christ of the Bible and the historic creeds and confessions, and theological liberals and radicals who for whatever reason do not; and this division splits the older Protestant bodies and the Roman Catholic communion equally, from the inside.

(*Evangelicals and Catholics Together*, pp.171-172)

The determination of some provinces to break fellowship with theological liberals and radicals is not a sign of divisiveness, but of their commitment to genuine catholicity, in the same way that Athanasius kept separate from the Arians for the sake of the unity of truth.

1.2.3   Charismatic

'You will receive power when the Holy Spirit has come upon you' (Acts 1:8). The Christian church from its very beginning is a charismatic church, waiting on God the Holy Spirit and ministering his gifts. While Anglicans have at times dismissed the manifestations of the Spirit as 'enthusiasm', and excluded movements like Methodism which sought to promote spiritual holiness, true Anglican orthodoxy recognises that the presence and power of the Holy Spirit are essential to its life and mission.

The Spirit is the engine of mission, sending out gospel witnesses to the ends of the earth. Anglicanism has had a mixed record in this regard. Much of the most effective mission work overseas was accomplished on the fringes of the Church of England, through voluntary societies. Nevertheless, the gospel did go out through hundreds of committed Anglican missionaries, many of whom paid the ultimate price for their calling. These missionaries laid a foundation that has been built on by the indigenous leaders of the Global South churches. Now these churches are themselves evangelizing the peoples within and across their national borders.

Anglicans have also been influenced by the spiritual revivals of the twentieth century. In East Africa, two types of spiritual dynamism emerged, the East African revival, flowing out of Rwanda in 1935, and the more recent Pentecostal and charismatic movements. The former movement emphasized the power of Christ's sacrificial death in relation to the believer; the latter emphasized the revitalizing of congregational worship and praise. Both of these have Western roots, but they have been indigenized and expressed in categories of traditional religion, including glossolalia, exorcism and prophecy.

1.3   Anglican orthodox discipline

Anglican orthodoxy was originally part of an 'Erastian' vision of a national church, established in English law. The first Lambeth Conference recognised that governance of the new churches of the empire was best achieved through a commitment to uniform faith and order, with discipline among the members being executed by national synods. Affirming this view, the bishops at Lambeth 1930 argued that in the extreme case of a member church diverging from this faith and order, 'formal action would belong to the several Churches of the Anglican Communion individually', with advice from the Lambeth Conference.

Roger Beckwith has noted (*Churchman* 2003, pp.359-361) that this system of governance resembles the way in which autonomous Eastern Orthodox churches exercise discipline, by excommunicating errant member churches. Beckwith argues that, in the current situation, with the so-called Instruments of Unity unwilling or unable to enforce Communion discipline in the matter of homosexuality, Anglican bishops and synods in the Global South have, perhaps unwittingly, adopted the Orthodox mode of inter-church discipline.

This is not to say that orthodox Anglican churches intend to splinter, with each 'doing what is right in his own eyes'. In 2002, they proposed a careful process of communal discipline, called *To Mend the Net*, only to see it disappear in the gears of the Communion bureaucracy. Again, the Global South Primates accepted the Archbishop of Canterbury's appeal, in 2003, to defer the disciplining of TEC for a year, only to have the 'Windsor process' drag on to Lambeth 2008 and beyond. Some continue to hope that an Anglican Covenant will result in a clear statement of orthodoxy, which will require the heterodox to conform or else walk apart. Others have concluded that the Covenant itself will be diluted and delayed, and that it is necessary, therefore, to come together with a renewed common vision of Anglican orthodoxy, free from the present distractions and machinations.

The central affirmation of Scripture, and of our Anglican Creeds, is that Jesus is Lord. What does this imply for our life and work? To this we turn.

2. The Lordship of Christ, in the Church and in mission

'Jesus is Lord' (1 Corinthians 12:3): this confession, which is only spoken as the result of the Holy Spirit's work in the heart of a believer, is fundamental to Christianity. The truth that Jesus is Lord also underpins and connects these two topics: the Lordship of Christ in the Church, and the Lordship of Christ in mission.

2.1 The Lordship of Christ in the Church

2.1.1   The Lordship of Christ and the Trinity

The truth that Jesus is Lord must itself be seen in the light of orthodox Christian belief: we believe in one living and true God, of one Substance and in three Persons, Father, Son and Holy Spirit, who exist in mutual indwelling love.

Indeed, the Bible tells us that in this indwelling network of love, the Father loves the Son. This is expressed by the voice from heaven at Jesus' baptism and also his transfiguration (Matthew 3:17 and 17:5) and asserted by Jesus himself (John 5:20). The Father shows his paternal generosity in at least three respects: first, providing the Son with a people; secondly, giving the Son, after his resurrection and ascension, Lordship over all things for all time, and thirdly, giving the Son authority to exercise judgement at his Second Coming. We shall investigate these gifts of the Father to the Son in turn.

Before we do so, we glory in the fact that this does not exhaust the account of love between the Persons of the Trinity. While the Father's love is shown in paternal generosity, Jesus the Son loves the Father; in the incarnation Jesus' obedience is grounded in his love for his Father (John 14:31). The Son loves as a son should, obeying his Father. Indeed, it is out of this love for his Father that Jesus the Son submits to being sent by his Father into the world (John 3:16), and takes human nature – as the Nicene Creed and Chalcedonian Definition express it – for us and for our salvation.

This eternal relationship of mutual love is reflected in the graciousness with which the triune God creates the cosmos from nothing, with blessing (Genesis 1:28, 2:3). It is also reflected in God's merciful act of saving sinful and enslaved human creatures, blessing them with the forgiveness of sins and also adoption (Ephesians 1:3-14).

2.1.2 The Father gives the Son a people (Colossians 1:13,14): Jesus the Deliverer[18]

St Paul writes:

> He [the Father] has rescued us from the power of darkness and transferred us into the kingdom of his beloved Son, in whom we have redemption, the forgiveness of sins. (Colossians 1:13,14) (NRSV)

This speaks of the time before we became Christians, a time when we were not free, but under an alien dominion, in fact an alien dominion characterized by darkness and death.

We can speak of this from an African and South American perspective, and also a Western one. In African and South American contexts the truth of Colossians 1:13f is evident in the struggle to rid men and women of the entanglement and entrapment of the powers of darkness.[19] Those under the oppressive

---

[18] See Michael Fape, *Powers in Encounter with Power* (Fearn, Ross-shire: Christian Focus Publications, 2003), chapter 7.

[19] Principalities and powers are real phenomena in the world, as African and South American theologians and believers recognise (see Michael Fape *op cit.* and Alfredo Neufeld, *Contra la Sagrada Resignación* (Asunción: El Lector, 2006). These may mean nothing to Westerners, but not so with other Christians. For instance, in the words of Peter O'Brien, 'Any study of the principalities and powers quickly runs into problems of language, for the apostle Paul (not to mention other New Testament writers) uses terminology that is strange to us ... The problem lies with many contemporary Western theologians and their cultural conditioning; they have allowed the latter to dictate their understanding of the biblical texts with the result that an increasingly fashionable view, viz., that the Pauline powers designate modern socio-political structures, has become the new orthodoxy'. P. T. O'Brien, 'Principalities and Powers: Opponents of the Church' in *Biblical Interpretation and the Church: Text and Context* (ed. D. A. Carson; Exeter: The Paternoster Press, 1984), p. 129. See also D. A. Carson, *The Gagging of God* (Michigan: Zondervan, 2002).

rule of demonic powers mainly turn to the gospel message in great distress, looking to find release and sure relief. This will bring in a reign of peace and the assurance of a more fulfilled life. But by demonstrating who Christ is for us today, within the African and South American contexts, we see God in action, subduing demonic forces that regularly put up a strong fight to keep their victims in perpetual custody.

The result that the preaching of the gospel produces among unbelievers, after their conversion, shows clearly that the Christian faith indeed gives the reality of true redemption. Christ, by his death on the cross (Colossians 1:13-15), carries out a rescue of those in bondage to demonic powers, delivers them from that bondage to oppression in the kingdom of darkness, and leads them to freedom in him. Being in Christ now, there is no longer anything to fear. Believers experience the reality of Hebrews 2:14-15 and the victory of Christ that these verses describe. When unbelievers are completely set free by the power of God, as Warneck has rightly noted,

> They no longer need to give up their cattle for sacrifices and festival; they are no longer compelled to involve themselves in debt to meet the demands of the priest; they are no longer afraid of the magicians and magic.[20]

Westerners will usually be far less conscious of the reality of spiritual warfare impinging on their daily lives. There is, in any event, a deep-rooted anti-supernaturalism in much Western thought (including an incredulity about biblical miracles), and Western ideals of autonomy resist the thought of being under any dominion. Yet the testimony of the Bible is that one may indeed be a child of Satan, in the Johannine sense of doing Satan's will (John 8:44), without consciously owning the fact but rather denying it (John 8:41, 48). And, in truth, Westerners certainly know the reality of not being able to do the good they should, and also of bondage to the wealth they have created, 'spirits oppressed by pleasure, wealth and care.'[21]

---

[20] John Warneck, *The Living Forces of the Gospel: Experiences of a Missionary in Animistic Heathendom* (London: Oliphant, Anderson & Ferrier, 1909), p. 234.
[21] 'Lord, for the years your love has kept and guided' by Timothy Dudley-Smith, 1926-

Yet the Father has transferred us to the kingdom of his Son, whom he loves. It is a kingdom of light and life. And this deliverance is to the kingdom of the one who redeems us. Redemption, in verse 14 of Colossians 1, is explained as the forgiveness of sins. This alerts us to two points.

First, our place under the alien dominion of darkness is no innocent victimhood. Victims and oppression certainly exist in the world, but a victim culture exists too, and its unhealthy nature has been well documented.[22] The risk, for the person who portrays himself simply in the role of victim, is that he feels justified in manipulating others, including God, while distorting the truth about his own fallenness. By contrast, an accurate account of human subjection to alien dominion must include mention of our own sin. A purely therapeutic view of the human problem is false, because it underplays the wonders of Jesus' actions for us: he saved us by his sacrificial, propitiatory death *while we were yet sinners* (Romans 5:8).

Secondly, our existence is now in another kingdom. Salvation does not mean complete autonomy, for salvation is incorporation into the community of the kingdom of the Son. But our king is the one who has died for us, and we are no longer under a dominion that brings us death. Yet this kingdom has kingly features, which has implications for its members. As members of the Son's kingdom, we are to show obedience and loyalty, for the Son is King, and as loyal subjects we look to the words he himself has spoken, or caused others of his servants to speak.

In this kingdom we are in unity with Christ and, because we are each in him, we are consequently in unity with each other (Ephesians 4:5). In this way our salvation is a salvation into a people, the new humanity who are in Christ and no longer in Adam. Being

---

[22] Karpman describes the Victim Triangle in his influential article, S. Karpman 'Fairy Tales and Script Drama Analysis', *Transactional Analysis Bulletin* (1968), vol. 7, no.26, pp.39-43. Lasch develops aspects of victim culture, in Christopher Lasch *The Culture of Narcissism* (New York: W.W. Norton, 1979). For consideration of some basic theological issues surrounding manipulation in a victim culture, see M. J. Ovey, 'Victim chic? The rhetoric of victimhood', *Cambridge Papers* (2006), no.15, part 1.

in the kingdom of Jesus is what marks us out as the people of God, the Church. Other major biblical motifs concerning the Church also stress the supremacy of Jesus Christ among his people: the Church is a temple whose chief cornerstone is Jesus; the Church is the bride of Christ, and the Church is the body of which Jesus is the head.

Our transfer from the kingdom of darkness to the kingdom of the Son is associated with the gracious, kindly work of the Holy Spirit, giving us hearts of flesh in place of hearts of stone. In this work God is pleased to use the instrument of his word written, which is a word both inspired by the Spirit and applied by him to our hearts.

The Spirit is himself linked with the gifts that the ascended and reigning Jesus gives to the Church. He confirms our identity as children of God and heirs (Galatians 4:6f), and himself intercedes for us (Romans 8:27) as well as endowing the people of God as he sees fit for their tasks of service in the kingdom of the Son.

2.1.3   *The Father gives the Son Lordship over all*

St Matthew records:

> And Jesus came and said to them, 'All authority in heaven and on earth has been given to me. Go therefore and make disciples of all nations, baptizing them in the name of the Father and of the Son and of the Holy Spirit, and teaching them to obey everything that I have commanded you. And remember, I am with you always, to the end of the age. (Matthew 28:18-20, NRSV)

The gift to the Son of 'all authority' means that there are enormous implications for the subjects of his kingdom.

First, Jesus' people have both a mandate and a responsibility to evangelise. They need no permission from any other authority, since all other authorities are themselves subject to the Lordship of Jesus, not independent of him, and certainly not higher than him. This matters a great deal at a time when states and cultures seek to restrain the message of the gospel, either by outright bans on Christian evangelism or by censoring some parts of biblical teaching. The scope of this mandate to evangelise is 'all nations': the good news of Christ's Lordship and salvation is not to be restricted by arbitrary human choice based on race, class, wealth, perceived importance, prestige, ability or potential.

Moreover, everyone who has received the gift of salvation, and been set free from the kingdom of darkness, is also commanded to be a faithful herald of the good news. This is a question of obedience.

We will briefly review the context in which this heralding of faith takes place. God's redemptive love reached its apex in Christ's death on the cross. But this is inseparable from the resurrection which authenticates Christ's victory over the power of death and sin. However, Christ promised that on his return to his Father the Holy Spirit would come, from the Father and the Son, as Comforter. And so Jesus' ascension inaugurates the ministry of the Holy Spirit, who continues the work of conviction, conversion and sanctification of believers, making them ready for the second coming of Christ. The Holy Spirit works remarkably in the *new man*, instilling in him a sense of urgency to pursue the task of evangelism, in obedience to the Great Commission, and promising that those who believe will be followed by 'signs' (Acts 2:19). And Christ, in the power of the Holy Spirit, has promised to be with his people to the end of the age (Matthew 28:20).

Secondly, Christ's people are constrained in what they say. They are commanded to teach people to obey '*everything* that I [Jesus] have commanded you'. And so we are to preach what Christ has mandated, *his* word rather than ours, and not, in our independent wisdom, more or less. Christ's people are properly seen as stewards of the apostolic faith that has been handed down. They have neither the authority nor the wisdom to re-write the words of Christ, in ways that may be more palatable to a disbelieving and sinful human heart. Such a move tragically robs the gospel of saving power, and means that those addressed in this way remain in the dominion of darkness. This duty to teach all that Christ commands goes beyond the simple proclamation of the gospel, for we are to make *disciples*. Hence the importance of, for example, the catechizing of new believers.[23]

---

[23] As with the Church of Nigeria's *Operation 1-1-3*.

Thirdly, in this obedience that Matthew 28:18 calls for, there can be no competing loyalty. This follows from the scope and the timing of the gift of authority to Jesus. The ascended Christ reigns *now* in this present age, despite its continuing rebellion, and over all. Thus competing authorities are even *now*, in reality, subject to Christ. No aspect of human life can claim to be independent of the reign of Christ: all, whether political, economic or artistic, is under him.[24] We therefore do not conform ourselves to this present age (compare Romans 12:2), for we are a pilgrim people, living in the present world, which we know is passing away, and looking beyond it to its true lord. We are prepared, if necessary, to give our lives now in anticipation of the world to come, which is the real world.

Fourthly, while the content of what Christ has entrusted to us is not ours to alter, modify, deny or add to, effective teaching presupposes effective communication within particular contexts. Authentic obedience to the Great Commission of Matthew 28 thus has a dynamic aspect, seeking apt ways to communicate in new historical and local situations, while safeguarding the deposit of faith itself. For, as a pilgrim people, we relate to, but are not conformed to, the present age.

Fifthly, Matthew 28:18-20 must also be seen in conjunction with the Lucan commission (Luke 24:47-48). The communication of the truth of Christ's kingship and his commands is not mere information, a piece of intellectual news to the effect that authority is now vested in Christ. Rather, it is a message containing a summons to repentance and also the offer of forgiveness. It presupposes a human race which, after Genesis 3, is predisposed against God, and whose rebellion and disbelief merit punishment and require forgiveness. The message of the cross is that Christ has purchased this forgiveness: he saves us from the wrath to come (1 Thessalonians 1:9,10).

---

[24] The view that each sphere of human activity in creation is properly subject to Jesus, because Christ is Lord of all creation, is expressed in *The Social Question and the Christian Religion* (1891), by Abraham Kuyper, the Dutch journalist, politician, statesman and theologian, and Prime Minister of The Netherlands 1901-1905.

2.1.4 The Father gives the Son authority to judge (John 5:22)

There is another, future, dimension to the Lordship that the Father gives to the Son. God in his goodness will one day set the world to rights, and this involves the execution of justice. God has given Jesus the prerogative to be the Judge of all at the end of the age. It is true that he came at first to be the 'Lamb of God who takes away the sin of the world' (John 1:29), but then he comes the second time to be the Judge of all, because the Father has given him all authority to judge men and women, for heaven or hell. Repentance is therefore commanded to all, so as to avoid Jesus condemning us as our Judge at his second coming (Acts 17:30). This is a day for which God's people are hoping, because Jesus comes to reign eternally in glory and justice at his second coming, and also because God in his mercy promises forgiveness to those who turn to God in repentance and faith. God's people are called on to wait in hope for that day (1 Thessalonians 1:10), to be on watch for it, and meanwhile to proclaim to others God's promise of mercy and to do works that befit those who 'belong to the day' (1 Thessalonians 5:8). We will consider, shortly, the deeds 'of the day' and the mission of the Church under the Lordship of Christ.

2.1.5 Summary

We have now seen the Lordship of Christ in the Church in three different dimensions. First, the Church is the kingdom of the Son, and God has transferred men, women and children into this kingdom, not into complete autonomy, or a spiritual republic. There are no people of God except in the kingdom of the Son. Secondly, Jesus the Son currently has all authority and, ascended, reigns now over the cosmos. His people recognise his authority on earth now; they do not simply look forward to the future reign of Christ. Thirdly, Jesus' people do look to the future consummation of this existing reality, when Jesus the Son will return to judge the world and finally deliver his people.

2.2 The Lordship of Christ in mission

2.2.1 Meeting the world

The world we meet is created by God and upheld by him in his providence and love. The signs of his continuing common grace bear witness to this. Yet the world is marred, diverse and complex. However, we meet this world in the light of the Lordship of Christ, and since a servant is not greater than his or her master, our encounter with the world must replicate the features of Jesus' encounter.

Our encounter with the world, over which Jesus is Lord, is marked by the knowledge that we and others are created by the triune God and, uniquely, created in his image. In our relationships with others, we realise that we are dealing with people who belong to God (Psalm 24:1,2), created by him for his purposes in creation. It is for this reason that we have a duty to treat others with respect, dignity and love (see Proverbs 14:31).

We know, too, that humanity has marred itself by sin, and enslaved itself, and that in this slavery humans treat each other not as creatures made in the image of God but as things, to be owned, used and exploited. We recognise, therefore, that the human world is one marked by victimization, as well as being marked by guilt before God.

We know, next, that there is an exclusivity to Christ's Lordship, such that humans cannot mix allegiances (1 Corinthians 10:14ff), seeking to serve two or more 'lords' (Jesus and Apollo, Jesus and Buddha, Jesus and hedonism). We also know that to deny this Lordship is to refuse salvation, since only the Lordship of Jesus will save a person.

We know, finally, that Jesus' Lordship is not only about saving people, but also about serving them. Of course we must serve by proclaiming the gospel, but the principle of neighbourliness (Luke 10:25-37) also requires more practical ways of help, what in a South American context would be referred to as *misión integral.* For, while he was here on earth, Jesus was concerned not only for the spiritual wellbeing of his audiences, but also for their physical needs, which he met with great compassion. In Matthew's account of the feeding of the five thousand (Matthew 14:13-21), it is interesting that, after preaching the good news to a multitude, Jesus commanded his *disciples* to give the people something to eat (verse 16), before providing the food himself.

2.2.2 Other faiths

These considerations mark the encounter of the people of God with other faiths. Remembering the truth of the words of Augustine – who also had to face a world of other faiths – that 'our heart is restless until it rests in you',[25] we can recognise that there is an authenticity to the spiritual restlessness and yearning for eternity and transcendence that many other faiths seek to meet, for we know that these things lie in the human heart. But authentic, saving, rest is only found in Jesus Christ. No one comes to the Father except through the Son (John 14:6).

Particular mention must be made of the Church's encounter with secularism. For secularism is the worldview that seeks to exclude the Lordship of Christ from this world; by denying there is any reality but the reality of this world, it denies any Lordship to Jesus. A Christian response is not to repudiate this world, for the world continues to be God's creation, containing signs of his goodness to us. Since Christians are *in* the world, though they do not belong to it, their lives should be a demonstration to the world of God's goodness and love, and the Church should offer ministries that, uniquely, bring the touch of heaven to earth. There is no question of compromising the faith in this. Our light must shine in the world, so that non-Christians see the good deeds of Christians and glorify the name of God (Matthew 5:16).

2.2.3 A world of need

The world we meet is also a world of pressing need, in many ways.

A primary area where the world needs the ministry of the Church is that of family and sexuality: 'Faithful and fruitful mission will include the protection and promotion of sound marriages, healthy families and holy singleness.'[26] For God has given us marriage and family life as gifts in creation (Genesis 2:18ff), elements of common grace for fallen humanity. Marriage manifests

---

[25] *Confessions* I.1
[26] Consultation Statement, 'Anglican Life in Mission', EFAC International Consultation July 2003, Limuru, Kenya. Printed in 'Anglican Life in Mission', *Transformation* 21/1 (January 2004): 7.

the equal value of men and women before God, and also their complementarity. Marriage between man and woman is the context in which the good (for God creates all things good), yet powerful (as the *Song of Songs* notes), gift of sexuality is to be cherished, respected and enjoyed. With respect to the family, this is the most basic unit of all social organizations, and is rightly called a micro-society. Without healthy family life, the life of society can only suffer.

Just as God, in creation, establishes the true purpose for human existence, so too he establishes the purposes for his gifts; these are to be enjoyed according to his commands. Thus, Genesis 2:18ff establishes the norm of monogamous heterosexual marriage for the exercise of the gift of sexuality. As with other gifts of God, this gift may be twisted to serve purposes other than those for which it was given. Such sinful distortions may occur in different ways in different cultures and places. We see with sadness the practice of polygamy in some African contexts, and we observe, too, the Western acceptance of serial monogamy, in which marriage is followed by casual divorce and subsequent re-marriage, not once but several times. South Americans may likewise feel that the ideal of Genesis 2:18ff has not been adequately presented within their cultures. But the biblical pattern for marriage, that it should be a lifelong relationship between a man and a woman, provides the context in which we must see the current issue, within the Anglican Communion, of homosexual practice or same-sex relations being described as marriage. A statement from the Province of the Southern Cone has rightly said:

> We affirm that ... adultery, sex outside of marriage and homosexual unions are all contrary to God's purposes for our humanity. We likewise deplore homophobia, hypocrisy and sexual abuse and seek to acknowledge and overcome such sins.[27]

A church which fails to call back to this norm (of Genesis 2:18ff) the culture to which it is sent, risks condemning both itself and the culture. It condemns itself because it is conforming to the world

---

[27] Quoted in 'Anglican Life in Mission', 7.

and not to the teaching that Jesus has commanded, and it condemns the culture, because the erosion of family life corrodes both the individual and the society of which he or she is a part.

In the area of health and social services, need will differ from one society or nation to another. In countries where people are living with HIV and AIDS, the church must continue to be an active participant because of the love and hope that lie at the heart of the gospel. The Church of Uganda's emphasis on behaviour change and other interventions has been rightly praised by those outside the church. Similarly the Church of Kenya has contributed remarkably, through its empowering educational programmes. Of great significance was the Provincial Action Committee on AIDS (PACA), an initiative of the Church of Nigeria, which was inaugurated in June 2004. Through this body, the church has been able to minister to the needs of local people in different parts of Nigeria, thereby making the church relevant to people when they are hurting, as well as educating them on the need for a well-guarded sexual life. We should mention, too, the pressing need to care for malaria sufferers, in view of the huge impact of this disease; in Kenya, more children die of malaria than AIDS. Elsewhere other troubles arise, such as the increase of tuberculosis in South America.

The principles we have looked at so far must be applied also to poverty, and some of the problems associated with it. If Christ is Lord, we must remember that he is lord of the economic sphere as well as everything else. But some groups and races – for example indigenous South Americans and some Aboriginal groups in Australia – remain effectively untouched by aid programmes. Defiance of Christ's laws in this sphere is no less serious than it would be in other areas of life, and just as we would speak against adultery, whoever did it, so too we should speak against exploitation and corruption. In the economic sphere, perhaps especially, the duty of being a good neighbour, in a way that is both loving and responsible, must be recognised. Both elements matter here: there is a pressing need to love one's neighbour, true, but there are ways of providing support and showing concern that are ultimately irresponsible, even if well-intentioned. We think, for instance, of the way that support to the poverty-stricken, both within individual nations and between nations, has sometimes helped create a demeaning culture of dependency, and perpetuated problems of vulnerability and indignity rather than solving them. Neighbourliness that is genuinely loving, moreover, may well display a different attitude in matters of development, exercising patience and looking less to self-interest.

In its mission to bring complete wholeness to society, the church needs to encourage members to gain financial independence. For this reason various churches are trying to initiate economic empowerment programmes, which enable Christians to get involved in productive economic ventures, without being worldly in implementation.

2.3 Epilogue

We have stressed that in the Church, and in the Church's mission to the world, Jesus is Lord. Such an assertion is sometimes thought to be a denial of love, in that Lordship and love are thought to be antithetical, contradictory notions. Yet Jesus himself is emphatic that love and Lordship *do* go together, and in two respects. We know that he loves us, for he gave himself for us, and yet he insists that he is our Lord. Also, he tells us that our love is to be shown in obedience to his commands (John 14:15; 2 John 6). This means that disobedience to what Jesus commands is a denial of love, for him, for his people, for the world.

In affirming obedience to Jesus as Lord, how should we expect his authority to be exercised, discerned, expressed and obeyed? To this we turn.

3. How do we know the truth about God, and his purposes?

The current crisis within the Anglican Communion is, in very large measure, generated by conflicting views on how Christians come to know God and his purposes. Just what is it that constitutes the final authority, when it comes to our ideas about God and what he is doing in the world? What determines how we ought to live, as those he has redeemed in Christ? Are these things to be determined by what seems reasonable to the larger culture in which we operate as Anglican Christians? Are the determinations of synods and ecclesiastical councils or conferences decisive? Are we to expect direct leadings of the Spirit, which make the right course of action seem intuitive? Or has God promised to make his mind known in some other way?

In recent years some have sought to redefine the answers to these questions, in ways which are deeply contrary to authentic Anglicanism as described in the Thirty-nine Articles, the Book of Common Prayer and the Homilies. This means that a fresh statement of the real nature of authority within authentic Anglicanism is urgently needed, as is a more explicit treatment of how we ought to approach the task of reading and explaining Scripture in the light of that statement. However, it is equally important that our consideration of this subject take a form which is consistent with its own conclusions. This will mean that it must be shaped by a rigorous biblical theology.

3.1 Christ, the authority in the Church

All authority in heaven and on earth has been given to Jesus Christ.[28] As Israel's Messiah and the eternal Son of the Father, he stands over all other claims to authority, however they might be constituted. He alone is the appointed judge of all human life and activity.[29] Every decision is subject to his scrutiny. He alone is the appointed saviour of the world, the only hope of all men and women, and his is the one name given under heaven by which we must be saved.[30] His lordship is the goal for which all things were made.[31] It is the great unchanging purpose of God the Father to bring all things together under the headship of God the Son by the powerful work of God the Spirit.[32] While many ignore or defy his authority at present, the day is most surely coming when every knee will bow and every tongue confess that Jesus Christ is Lord, and this cannot help but demonstrate the glory of God the Father.[33]

More specifically, Jesus Christ is the only head of the Church.[34] He is the one who is building his Church and not even the gates of Hades can prevail against it.[35] No human consensus or claim to institutional legitimacy can be grounds to modify or set aside his rule in even the most minute measure. The Church is forever dependent on Christ. He is present as his people gather in his name, just as he promised.[36] He poured out his Spirit on his people on the Day of Pentecost and by this same Spirit he gives gifts to his people today so that they might serve each other and grow into his likeness.[37] Believers are exhorted to let his word dwell in them richly.[38] Christian discipleship is fundamentally a recognition of Christ's lordship, his right to direct the life and thought of the

---

[28] Matthew 28:18.
[29] Acts 17:30-31.
[30] Acts 4:12; Ephesians 2:12; John 14:6.
[31] Colossians 1:16.
[32] Ephesians 1:10.
[33] Philippians 2:10-11.
[34] Ephesians 5:23.
[35] Matthew 16:18.
[36] Matthew 18:20.
[37] Acts 2:32-33; Ephesians 4:11-14; 1 Corinthians 12:4-7.
[38] Colossians 3:16.

redeemed people of God. There can be no Church where the authority of Christ to call us to faith and repentance – to challenge our cultural commitments, our personal preferences and our traditions – is neglected.

Christ exercises this authority in the churches throughout these last days by his word through his Spirit. Just as during his earthly ministry Jesus' words stilled the storm, expelled the demons, healed the sick and raised the dead, so today they nourish faith and direct the lives of those who follow him.[39] Jesus leads his people today by his word addressed to them as his disciples. Likewise, the Spirit who rested upon Jesus throughout his earthly ministry attends his word today, transforming lives by that word as men and women are convicted and convinced of its truth.[40] Faith, that genuine confidence and trust in Christ's good word which gives rise to a wholehearted obedience, is the result of the Spirit's work in the human heart.[41] In this way it becomes clear that the word and the Spirit are not to be considered as two separate and potentially competing means, by which the living and active Christ operates in the Church over its long history. Christ rules by his word through his Spirit.

This is seen most clearly in the Scriptures. The Old Testament is the written form of the word of God carried on the breath of God.[42] The apostolic writings share this same character, by virtue of Christ's promise and commission.[43] The Bible lies at the centre of the Church's life precisely because it is the Spirit-inspired written form of the word of God, by which Christ's authority is exercised until he returns.[44] These Scriptures are not limited in truth and relevance because they were spoken in the first century, nor are they bound by time, culture or space. Rather, they express the mind of God who knows all things as they truly are. This is why

---

[39] E.g. Mark 4:35-41; 9:14-29; 1:40-45; 5:35-43.
[40] John 16:7-15.
[41] John 3:1-8; Ephesians 2:8-9; 3:14-19; 2 Corinthians 4:13-14.
[42] 2 Timothy 3:16-17; 2 Peter 1:20-21.
[43] John 14:15-26; Matthew 28:18-20; 2 Peter 3:15-16.
[44] See the following subsection of this document for further discussion of the nature and origin of Scripture, and the consequences for both its place in the church and the way it is read by Christians.

they are never dated or outmoded. They never need to be corrected in the light of new advances in knowledge. Rather, they remain eternally relevant and authoritative. Yet the Scriptures are not an alternative to the dynamic personal presence of Christ, the Church's Lord. By his word and through his Spirit he is present 'until the end of the age'.

Any other authority exercised amongst God's people must be subject to the authority of Christ, and so subject to the authority of the Scriptures. The authority in the Church, exercised on behalf of Christ, can only be authority that is subject to the teaching of the Bible as the written word of God. The doctrine and lifestyle of all who exercise leadership among the churches is to be tested by the teaching of Scripture, as was the case with the apostles themselves.[45] There is no place in Christian leadership for those who are committed to patterns of behaviour on account of which 'the wrath of God is coming'.[46] Furthermore, the manner of leadership among the churches is likewise to be tested against the example of Christ, as attested in the Scriptures. Obedience, and a determination to serve rather than to dominate, are the constituent elements of that genuine humility the churches are to expect in all who lead according to the pattern of Christ.[47] Such leaders (no matter how exalted their title or claim to jurisdiction) do not stand over the Scriptures, determining what is acceptable today and what is not. Instead they sit under the Scriptures, prepared to be challenged and corrected themselves by the written word of God. Repentance in the light of the teaching of Scripture is to be a constant characteristic of their lives. They forfeit the authority that has been delegated to them when this is not the case. This is, tragically, much more than simply a hypothetical reality. The need to stand against false teaching and the abuse of authority within the churches, throughout the entire period until the Lord returns, is anticipated by Jesus himself and by his apostles.[48]

A similar dynamic is at work in confessional statements,

---

[45] Acts 17:10-11; Galatians 2.
[46] Ephesians 5:5-6; Colossians 3:5-6.
[47] Mark 10:42-45; Philippians 2:3-11.
[48] Matthew 24:3-14; 1 Timothy 6:3-10; 2 Timothy 3:1-5.

such as the Thirty-nine Articles of Religion. These are genuinely authoritative documents, but their authority is always dependent upon their faithful reflection of the teaching of Scripture as the word of the Church's only Lord. This is explicitly recognised, in the case of the Thirty-nine Articles, by Articles VI, VII and XX, while Article VIII makes the same point with reference to the ancient Creeds. The interpretative grid against which the Articles are to be read is the teaching of Scripture, just as the Articles are presented as an attempt to distil that teaching on a number of important issues. The words, grammar and historical context of the Articles make clear that they have a real but contingent authority, arising as they do in a world where Councils and other ecclesiastical assemblies 'may err and sometimes have erred, even in things pertaining unto God'.

While it is sometimes said that the three-legged stool of Scripture, tradition and reason is a mutually referring and informing authority for Anglicans – a concept usually but inaccurately attributed to comments by Richard Hooker in his *Of the Lawes of Ecclesiastical Polity* – the idea, in fact, finds no support in Scripture, nor in the foundational documents of Anglicanism (The Thirty-nine Articles, The Book of Common Prayer and The Homilies). Scripture stands alone, above both the tradition of the churches and the carefully reasoned arguments of the human mind.[49] The Christian tradition is not to be despised or treated lightly, but it is always reformable on the basis of biblical teaching. And human reason is a gift of God, which remains useful even on this side of the Fall. It is actively employed in the reading of Scripture. However, it too needs reformation by the teaching of Scripture. In contrast Scripture, as the written word of God, needs no reformation or correction, either by the consensus of Christians or by the fresh insights of human reason.

On occasion, departures from biblical teaching have been justified by appeal to the notion of prophecy. Those who advocate innovation in Christian thought and practice insist that their

---

[49] This is in fact what Hooker taught: 'What Scripture doth plainly deliver, to that *the first place of credit* and obedience is due; *the next* whereunto is whatever any man can necessarily conclude by force of reason; *after these* the voice of the church succeedeth.' Hooker, *Lawes,* V.8.2.

proposals are a new word from the Spirit. However, in the Old Testament and in the New, claims to possess new prophetic words are not self-authenticating; the new prophetic words are to be tested for their consistency with the teaching of the Scriptures.[50] A truly prophetic word not only 'comes to pass' in the world, it also reflects the teaching of the Bible. True prophets call people back to the words that God has already spoken, demanding faith and repentance. Precisely because 'many false prophets have gone out into the world', all proposals need to be tested by the Scriptures.[51] Testing even the words of the apostles by the teaching of the Scriptures is commended in the New Testament.[52]

3.2 The nature of Scripture, and its use in the Church

The canonical Scriptures of the Old and New Testaments are the written word of God. At the same time they are self-evidently human texts, using human words penned by human beings in particular historical, cultural and linguistic contexts. Both of these dimensions must be affirmed with equal seriousness. Human beings moved by the Holy Spirit spoke from God, and the result was texts which are God-breathed.[53] The ultimate origin of these texts in the breath of God does not do away with the significance of the contribution made by each human author and the various contexts in which they wrote. The human authors were consciously and creatively involved as they were moved by the Spirit. Likewise, the genuine humanity of these texts is no impediment to their communication of God's thoughts, words and personal presence. These words, 'written for our instruction' by those God himself commissioned in various ways, indelibly bear the unchangeable and unchallengeable authority of God.[54]

Jesus Christ himself treated the Old Testament Scriptures as the word of God, upholding them as authoritative Scripture which ends all speculation about the nature, character and purposes of

---

[50] Deuteronomy 13:1-5.
[51] 1 John 4:1-6.
[52] Acts 17:11.
[53] 2 Peter 1:19-21; 2 Timothy 3:16-17.
[54] Romans 15:4.

God. His appeal to the Old Testament during the temptation in the wilderness demonstrates his assessment that these words were the appropriate and final answer to the challenges posed by the ancient enemy, in stark contrast to the way the first man and woman responded to a similar challenge.[55] He regularly made a similar appeal to the words of the Old Testament in his debates with the religious leaders of his day. They ought to have read and heeded the 'word of God' – an expression he saw no need to qualify when used of an Old Testament text – and he considered it scandalous that they should set this word aside in the interests of human tradition.[56]

Jesus consistently characterised the Old Testament Scriptures as the authoritative testimony to his person and mission. They all point to him, they are fulfilled in him, and they provide the proper categories for understanding what he came to do.[57] While Jesus' own use of the Old Testament assumes a basic unity for its various texts, which is properly traced to their common origin in the breath of God, he explicitly identifies this additional unity of reference: a common testimony to God's unfolding purpose, which has now come to its climax in his own life, work and words.

It is the commission of Jesus which generates the New Testament Scriptures. He gave a particular authority to his apostles to bear witness to him, just as over the centuries the writings of the prophets had borne witness to him.[58] He promised them the Holy Spirit, who would remind them of all he had told them while he was amongst them.[59] The testimony which the Spirit would enable them to bear to Jesus was to extend 'to the end of the earth' and 'until the end of the age'.[60] The apostolic writings flow out of that commission. They are part of the discharge of the apostles' responsibility to proclaim Christ and his gospel 'to the Jew first and also to the Greek'.[61] As such they bear the authority of the Lord who commissioned the apostles and are rightly considered amongst 'the

---

[55] Matthew 4:1-11; cf. Genesis 3:1-7.
[56] Matthew 15:1-9.
[57] John 5:39; Luke 4:16-21; Mark 10:45; Luke 22:1-23.
[58] Luke 24:44-48; John 15: 27; Acts 1:8.
[59] John 14:25-26.
[60] Acts 1:8; Matthew 28:18-20.
[61] Romans 1:14-17.

other Scriptures'.[62]   Later discussion of the New Testament canon would make much of the apostolic provenance of these particular books and letters.   Far from investing the New Testament with authority, the decisions of the churches in the first few centuries acknowledged an authority which was prior to all ecclesiastical deliberation.   The New Testament is Christian Scripture alongside the Old Testament, not first and foremost because the churches received it as such, but because here is the apostolic testimony to Christ and the shape of life lived as his disciples.   The Scriptures are not the product of the churches.   Rather, Christ continues to address the churches by these words.

As an expression of this discipleship, all Christians and authentic Christian churches should delight in reflecting the attitude of their Lord to the Scriptures.   The reading and exposition of the Scriptures is a prominent feature of our gatherings, precisely because these are the words Jesus taught us to embrace as the gift of our loving Father, given to nourish the faith of his people.   God's own nature and character provide the guarantee of their goodness and effectiveness.   The authority, unity, clarity and sufficiency of the Scriptures arise directly from the sovereignty and benevolence of the holy God whose written word they are.

For this reason, a faithful reading of Scripture cannot approach the biblical text with suspicion or with the intention of exposing error, contradiction or irrelevance.   Such attitudes toward Scripture amount to an assault upon the character of the God who has given us this good word.   The Christian assumption is always that our problems with the teaching of Scripture are our problems, rather than problems with the Bible.   We have all been profoundly influenced by the Fall, in our reasoning as in every other area of our lives.   Cultural bias, a sense of historical superiority, and the intellectual expressions of a deep-seated human rebellion against the rule of God through his word, can combine with our ignorance of the whole of Scripture – and our lack of attention to what is actually said in the parts we do know – to produce sophisticated manipulations of the text in our own interests, or else a self-satisfied

---

[62]   2 Peter 3:15-16.

agnosticism. It is possible actually to evade the teaching of Scripture while giving others the impression that you are taking it very seriously, 'having the appearance of godliness but denying its power'.[63]

It is only by careful attention to, and reflection upon, the Scriptures that we are able to 'test everything [and] hold fast what is good'.[64] As with every other aspect of the Christian life, in both its individual and its corporate dimensions, this faithful, attentive reflection can only be done in prayerful dependence upon the Holy Spirit. The same Spirit who was critically involved in the production of the biblical text enables us to adopt the appropriate stance as we read it. By his enabling, Christians are to read the Scriptures as disciples eager to learn, concerned to have our thinking and behaviour corrected, so that our lives might conform more truly to the ultimate reality of God's character and purposes. In short, Christians sit humbly under the Spirit-inspired Scriptures, desiring to live holy lives as Christ's disciples.

This careful attention to the Bible involves being directed by its purpose. Mistakes can and have been made when the Bible has been read either as a scientific text, concerned to expound principles of cosmology, geology, biology and the like, or as a narrative which provides an imaginative world, against which background we come to our own conclusions about what is valuable in human life and relationships. Instead, the purposes for which Scripture was given are explicit within Scripture itself. These include: to testify to Jesus Christ with the purpose of eliciting faith and repentance; to make those who read them 'wise for salvation through faith in Christ Jesus'; to instruct us so that 'through endurance and through the encouragement of the Scriptures we might have hope'; and to teach, reprove, correct and train in righteousness so that Christ's disciples might be 'competent, equipped for every good work'.[65]

Likewise, mistakes can be made when the Bible is read idiosyncratically or individualistically, with little or no regard for the communion of saints which provides the proper context for a

---

[63] 2 Timothy 3:5.
[64] 1 Thessalonians 5:21.
[65] John 5:39; 20:30-31; 2 Timothy 3:14-15; Romans 15:4; 1 Corinthians 10:11; 2 Timothy 3:16-17.

faithful approach to Scripture. Traditional readings of Scripture may need to be challenged, because they involve a mis-step at the point of understanding the words, their context or their purpose. Conventional readings are not proper readings simply because they are conventional. However, novelty has no special privileges either. The traditional interpretation of a text must not be lightly challenged or flippantly overthrown. None of us is the first to read the Scriptures with care, humility and faith. Special care needs to be taken when a proposed new reading results in an endorsement of the culture in which we live. It is all too easy to echo the world's commitments, rather than challenge them.

A critical element of the faithful reading of Scripture is a due regard for its unity and coherence. The practice of comparing Scripture with Scripture guards against fragmentary readings which frequently misuse individual texts. Biblical theology – the study of the unfolding nature of God's revelation in salvation history, which highlights the relationship of each part of the Bible to its centre in the person, words and work of Jesus Christ – is immensely valuable in this regard. It expresses the conviction that Scripture is its own interpreter, that one of the most important resources God has given us to understand any part of the Bible is the whole Bible. Faithful Christian doctrine and ethics rely upon both an explicit appeal to biblical texts, and an understanding of how those texts fit within the message of the Bible as a whole. This is also the commitment which lies behind the statement in Article XX of the Thirty-nine Articles of Religion: 'And yet it is not lawful for the Church to ordain any thing that is contrary to God's Word written, neither may it so expound one place of Scripture, that it be repugnant to another'.

The word of God is given to the people of God. It is not the private possession of either a scholarly elite or any ecclesiastical hierarchy. The New Testament insistence upon the public reading of Scripture[66] assumes that the plain meaning of Scripture is accessible to all, and that it nourishes the faith of believers regardless of cultural differences or educational background. God is actively involved as we read Scripture today, transforming lives in

---

[66] I Thessalonians 5:27; I Timothy 4:13.

the present as in the past through the powerful words which he has spoken, and which he caused to be written for the benefit of his people. The principal requirement is that we should be those who 'hear the word of God and keep it'.[67]

There is still a valuable place for the work of biblical and theological scholarship. It should not be dismissed as irrelevant, particularly when it encourages a careful reading of the text we have been given, and alerts us to features we might otherwise have missed. However, care must be taken not to position biblical scholarship as a new *magisterium*, an authoritative interpretation that is necessary if anyone is to understand the Bible. God addresses his people directly in the words of Scripture, conveyed to their hearts by his Spirit. He is able to convey clearly and effectively his message of salvation through the death and resurrection of Jesus Christ, together with his call to faith and holy living in the light of what Jesus has done.

In the light of our affirmations of the Lordship and the authority of Jesus Christ as the Son of God, how are we to worship God the Father through him, in the power of the Spirit and in truth? To this we turn.

---

[67] Luke 11:28.

4. Engaging with the Anglican liturgical heritage in shaping the future

Let us all enter into the joy of the Lord! [68]

4.1 Introduction to Anglican worship

Anglican worship goes back to the Reformation and, through the Reformation, to the early church and the Bible. The Book of Common Prayer, which Archbishop Cranmer devised at the time of the Reformation, was not a new thing, but it was new in many ways. It introduced worship in the vernacular, for instance, but it inherited from the past many edifying elements of worship, and took the Bible as the norm by which to judge what to maintain and what to discard. One result of this is to be found in the exhortation at the beginning of Morning and Evening Prayer, which sets out what the service is intended to contain: thanksgiving, praise, the reading of Scripture and prayer, all in the context of repentance and forgiveness.

4.1.1 We are a liturgical people

Anglican worship is designedly liturgical in order to restrain the Church from going astray in the way it approaches God. Anglican worship is also corporate in its intention, as the title 'Book of *Common* Prayer' implies, and it is normally led by the ordained ministry, but Christians are fully expected and encouraged to worship in private as well as in public. In order to prepare people for corporate worship, the first of the long exhortations before Holy Communion in the Prayer Book reminds them about what they are doing: they have come together to receive 'the Sacrament of the Body and Blood of Christ', which they will do 'in remembrance of his meritorious Cross and Passion; whereby alone we obtain remission of our sins, and are made partakers of the kingdom of

---

[68] *A Paschal Sermon*, by St John Chrysostom (347-407).

heaven.' It goes on to stress the great importance of confessing their sins and obtaining God's forgiveness before receiving the blessed Sacrament, for 'it is requisite, that no man should come to the holy Communion, but with a full trust in God's mercy, and with a quiet conscience.'

4.1.2   We have a ministry of word and sacrament

The Anglican ministry is a ministry of both word and sacraments, and both elements have a very prominent place in Prayer Book worship. The word enacted in sacrament is also a way in which people experience Christ. Article XIX of the Thirty-nine Articles lays down that one of the marks of the visible church is that the sacraments are rightly administered. This makes the Eucharist central to the liturgical life of the church. It is important to recognise that the heritage of the Prayer Book faith and formularies has left us with a rich and full doctrine of the Eucharist, with a strong sense of the presence of Christ, or 'real participation' to use the language of Hooker, and understanding of the nature of his sacrifice.

4.1.3   We uphold the Creeds and our historic formularies, believing in 'one holy, catholic and apostolic Church'

Anglican liturgy upholds its inheritance of the faith 'uniquely revealed' in the Scriptures which contain all things necessary for salvation. This faith is 'set forth' in the Creeds received by the whole church and recited in our liturgy. These three historic Creeds, being proved 'by most certain warrants of holy Scripture', were thus retained in the Prayer Book and they are reaffirmed in the Thirty-nine Articles (Article VIII) before these go on to speak of the other biblical truths which were highlighted at the Reformation.

Anglicans uphold the teaching of the Councils of the early undivided church, and the ecumenical norms of church order set out in the Lambeth Quadrilateral. It is timely to recall, given the great contribution of Africans in Alexandria and elsewhere to the early church, that Anglicans have characteristically appealed to the consensus of antiquity and the voice of the patristic church, in support of scriptural interpretation. Affirming together our shared assent to the fundamental articles of faith is what provides the necessary and sufficient conditions for Communion. To break from affirming the common faith and mind of the church is to fall short of these conditions for Communion and to step away from the fullness of true Christian fellowship.

The 1930 Lambeth Conference, in setting out the ideals for which the Anglican church has always stood, stressed features that were not held to be unique to Anglicanism but rather to be 'the ideals of the Church of Christ' including 'an open Bible, a pastoral priesthood, a common worship', and 'a standard of conduct consistent with that worship and a fearless love of truth'.

Anglicans, through their commitment to membership of the *holy*, catholic and apostolic Church, are committed to upholding that holiness of life and morals which Holy Scripture sets forth and requires. Our liturgy daily reminds us of this call to holiness and amendment of life. Doctrine and morals thus come together continually in the worship of the church; they do not stand apart from each other. 'Let your light so shine before men, that they may see your good works, and glorify your Father which is in heaven' (Matthew 5:16).

4.1.4 *We follow a liturgical calendar, a lectionary and a Catechism*

Anglicans retain a calendar of the Christian year as a means of recalling the life of our Lord and Saviour, and as a means of setting out the great truths of the gospel in turn each year. The calendar gives a pattern to Christian worship throughout the year. Archbishop Cranmer passed on to the Anglican church an historic lectionary with roots in the early church. The Sunday reading of Scripture was intended to ensure an orderly and doctrinally-based reading of Scripture, and the daily lectionary was designed to ensure that as much as possible of the Bible was read to congregations in their own language, every year. These aims should continue to inform such new lectionaries as Anglicans develop.

An important element in the Prayer Book was the Catechism, designed to teach the basic elements of Christian faith and worship to candidates for confirmation. A fuller Catechism was later provided, to give additional instruction. Further Catechisms may well be developed today, in continuity with this historic and biblical faith, as an aid in mission, and as a way of enhancing the effective teaching of the faith and encouraging its ever wider propagation.

4.1.5   We worship the Lord in spirit and in truth

Anglican worship, with its unifying Prayer Book tradition and biblical emphasis, has clearly upheld the benefits and dignity of the 'said prayers' and liturgy, yet we also recognise that freedom of worship that is truly in the Spirit is also an essential element of Christian life and devotion.   This element has sometimes been neglected in our tradition, and we therefore welcome the openness of approved contemporary liturgies to times for spontaneous prayer, prophecy, discernment of spirits, and testimony, within the framework of ordered liturgical worship. We recognise too the need for prayerful discernment in the light of our heritage of faith and practice, and subject to biblical norms. We believe that the Church, in the power of the Spirit, will manifest his gifts decently and in order, and with power and reverence.

4.2 The challenges of the present

O come, let us sing unto the Lord: let us heartily rejoice in the strength of our salvation. (Psalm 95, the *Venite*)

Worship is rooted in our faith in God's work of creation, incarnation and redemption, and we seek to enter more deeply into God's life and love as those who are called to be 'partakers of the divine nature' (2 Peter 1.4). 'The visible Church of Christ is a congregation of faithful men,' states Article XIX, 'in the which the pure Word of God is preached, and the Sacraments be duly administered according to Christ's ordinance'. Thus are we called, as Anglicans, to an ever deeper understanding of our heritage of structured and orderly corporate worship and private prayer, together with constant proclamation of God's word. It is in this work as God's people – which is his body, the Church – that our identity is both formed and expressed.

We invoke the Holy Spirit as we seek to be open to God's future, and to orient ourselves ever more fully to the fulfilment of God's will. We are bound together by the bonds of shared faith and common heritage, as we seek to be one in the Lord. Our worship and liturgy, which we have received, carry the historic faith of the church forward into the future, and in this way they challenge us to be true to our history, as evangelical, catholic and reformed. In particular, the great gift of the Book of Common Prayer is one that we continue to value, for it has done so much to define and shape the liturgy, faith and witness of our church. This is the heritage we must deepen and renew.

4.2.1 Daily prayer

We are enjoined 'to pray without ceasing', and the regular daily cycle of psalms and prayer, the reading of God's word and the singing of his praises, allows us to stand with Christ in unity with the Church of the ages. How can this heritage of morning and evening prayer be deepened and revived? How can the use of the Canticles and the recitation (musical chant) of the psalms best be renewed?

4.2.2 The Eucharist

The Eucharist, instituted by Christ himself, stands alone as the one great liturgical act which transcends all of time, bringing us into the great mystery which is Christ's once-for-all act of salvation. Holy Communion, as the central liturgical act of the church, must receive due emphasis in our worship, without it excluding other important daily elements such as those of Morning and Evening Prayer.

4.2.3 Some current challenges

A number of critical matters need to be addressed, as we seek to go forward in mission in ways that are both faithful and renewed.

How can Anglican liturgy best provide worship that leads us, both as a community and as individuals, to the experience of the transcendent and triune God, the Father, the Son and the Holy Spirit? How can Anglicans best come to see worship as that which leads to holiness, and to an encounter with the holy God who calls us to be transformed in Christ?

How can we best facilitate the effective hearing of God's word, and ensure that we 'read, mark, learn and inwardly digest' it? How can congregations be better nurtured in the word? How can worship best contribute to the continuing work of formation in the Christian life, to the fostering of holiness, and to a deep experience of God that will cause us to go out in mission?

Where is the Holy Spirit, and the spirit of celebration, encounter and response, in our worship? And how do we address the issues regarding our right discernment in the Spirit?

4.3   The future of Anglican worship

4.3.1   Building on the Prayer Book tradition

We will, as Anglicans, continue to cherish the Book of Common Prayer, mindful of its warning, in the section entitled 'Concerning the Service of the Church', that 'There was never any thing by the wit of man so well devised, or so sure established, which in continuance of time hath not been corrupted'.   The work of Cranmer, in crafting the Prayer Book, provided a bridge to the ancient worship of the Church, which had adapted but not changed the heritage of Christian teaching informed by Holy Scripture. The Anglican *future* in worship lies in maintaining this theology and this approach, rather than pursuing a particular style, and also in the comprehensive task of holding on to all that is Scriptural and in the best of our tradition, as we believe and obey the Lord.

4.3.2   Continuity and adaptation

The matter of style should not be settled simply according to present-day patterns, just as, in the past, it has not been settled according to biblical tradition alone.   Instead, style in worship should reflect an encounter with the culture of a given time and place.   The styles of Anglican worship will reflect who we are, peoples of one faith, and living in a multicultural, worldwide Communion.   Yet there will be a family resemblance that will mark us out as Anglican.   Cranmer had this in mind when he formulated Article XXXIV, stating that 'It is not necessary that Traditions and Ceremonies be in all places one, and utterly like'.   Nonetheless, we must not offend 'against the common order of the Church'. Forms of worship, therefore, are not to be imposed upon a people, which means that there is something refreshing and enriching about the diversity within our tradition.

In the future, Anglican worship should flourish if Anglicans continue to use their worship as an instrument of mission.   In many situations, the regular repetition of the Anglican liturgy has been the principal means of teaching the faith in illiterate communities.   This reminds us that worship is not dependent upon an elaborate intellectual grasp of the faith, and that the oral heritage of familiar and memorized prayers and texts, that we carry with us throughout our lives, is of the greatest value. So that it continues to be an instrument of mission, we must ensure that Anglican worship is always accessible to everyone, especially to children – 'From the lips of children and infants you have ordained praise' (Psalm 8:2) – and this would include the Eucharist itself.

Christians from all the Anglican provinces and dioceses can use their worship to bless other Christians, and the Anglican Communion, as they share what they have experienced of Christ, and also the way they have engaged in ministry in their local contexts. Music, of course, will help us in this.

4.3.3   The gift of music – enculturation and development

God's great gift to us of music poses a challenge: how should we best employ it, knowing as we do that it is subject to cultural forces? Athanasius warned of the dangers of using artistic forms that are not capable of conveying divine truth. Music can be a vehicle of self-expression in many situations, but how can we use music in worship in such a way that it moves us, but does not leave us merely focused upon ourselves and our present enjoyment? Christian liturgy is inherently musical, and music may be used both to evoke and to express the feelings of worshippers. The Anglican liturgical tradition, in particular, helps us to remember the role of music as a vehicle for conveying God's majesty and compassion, as well as the great acts and truths of the faith. Yet it is clear that mere observance of a set formula will not create a living and authentic celebration of worship.

Music is always placed within a wider liturgical context, whether it be that of hearing God's word, a celebration of the Eucharist, Morning or Evening Prayer, or some other occasional service. The psalms and canticles with their antiphons, the hymns, responsories, litanies, acclamations, greetings and responses, and even the prayers, may all be greatly enhanced by music and by being sung.

It is important to preserve the overall integrity of the entire experience of worship, prayer and devotion. The various component elements in worship must therefore cohere with, and be subservient to, the wider whole, and be appropriate to the solemnity or festivity of the occasion. It is not appropriate to impose private meanings upon public worship, and this discipline applies as much to musical performance and performers as to anything else. The music employed must be fitting and conducive to worship, and not a distraction or impediment.

According to the local context, different languages will be appropriate, so that the people present will understand and connect with all that takes place in worship. Anything less would be contrary to the clear statement in Article XXIV: 'It is a thing plainly repugnant to the Word of God, and the custom of the Primitive Church, to have publick Prayer in the Church, or to minister the Sacraments in a tongue not understanded of the people.' The same thing might be said about different *styles* in worship, though here the issue would be enrichment, rather than understanding. Pastoral sensitivity will guide as to the needs of the people in a particular context. Classical hymnody, and Anglican psalm chant and responsorial singing, should continue to have their place as part of the great Anglican musical and choral tradition of excellence that has come down to us. We should also embrace contemporary music for our services, and local cultural traditions too, while seeking to maintain at all points the goal of excellence, remembering always that our music is an offering to God.

4.3.4 *Future challenges*

How can we best ensure the renewal of Anglican traditions of musical excellence? And how can we best engage with earlier, indigenous Christian traditions in music and liturgy, especially in places where ancient traditions continue in Anglican worship today? This is the case with the Coptic liturgy of St Basil, to name but one example. It should be remembered that Cranmer was influenced to some extent by the Eastern Orthodox liturgy, and later on the Liturgy of St John Chrysostom was to influence Lancelot Andrewes. Today, what can we learn from our differing church experiences of musical and liturgical practice? In recent times, for example, the worship of the churches in North and South India has reflected elements from the earlier Rites of Bombay and Ceylon (Sri Lanka). What examples of excellence, from our many and various local contexts, could we share with each other?

How can we ensure that Anglican worship connects with the needs of the modern world? The diversity of patterns of worship, coming from around the Communion, includes occasional services – liturgies, benedictions and celebrations for the different stages of life's journey, from the cradle to the grave, and in accord with local needs. Liturgies must always speak to pastoral need, but the Book of Common Prayer of 1662 does not have everything that every context requires! Using modern technology, Anglicans can make available additional resources – obtained through appropriate mutual consultation, and with permission – so that sister churches and other Christian communities may better minister to a hurting world. Many other churches look to Anglicans for such resources, but Anglicanism itself has been blessed by the many and varied resources of others. The bands and processions of the Salvation Army, for instance, offer a vivid example of music being used in outreach.

We need many and varied resources to use in mission, as tools of ministry. In future, provision may be required to meet special liturgical needs. In an African context, these needs might include specific provision for rites of passage, and occasional services for special events, such as family and community occasions, agricultural seasons, and even industrial 'fixtures'. Of particular importance is the need to provide services with and for children; it is vital that children be truly and fully incorporated into the worshipping life of the Church.

4.4 The unchanging goal of bringing all to Christ

It is fitting to close this section with the words of Archbishop Cranmer himself, for they most eloquently disclose the force and urgency that lie behind our Anglican heritage, in liturgy and worship, as it seeks to bring all to Christ:

> When we hear Christ speak unto us with his own mouth, and shew himself to be seen with our eyes, in such sort as is convenient for him of us in this mortal life to be heard and seen; what comfort can we have more? The minister of the Church speaketh unto us God's own words, which we must take as spoken from God's own mouth, because that from

his mouth it came, and his word it is, and not the minister's.

Likewise, when he ministereth to our sights Christ's holy sacraments, we must think Christ crucified and presented before our eyes, because the sacraments so represent him, and be his sacraments, and not the priest's; as in baptism we must think, that as the priest putteth his hand to the child outwardly, and washeth him with water, so we must think that God putteth his hand inwardly and washeth the infant with his holy Spirit; and moreover, that Christ himself cometh down upon the child, and appareleth him with his own self: and at the Lord's holy table the priest distributeth wine and bread to feed the body, so we must think that inwardly by faith we see Christ feeding both body and soul to eternal life. What comfort can be devised any more in this world for a Christian man?[69]

---

[69] Thomas Cranmer, *An Answer by the Reverend Father in God, Thomas, Archbishop of Canterbury, Primate of all England, and Metropolitan, unto a Crafty and Sophistical Cavillation, devised by Stephen Gardiner, Doctor of Law, late Bishop of Winchester, against the true and godly doctrine of the most Holy Sacrament, of the Body and Blood of our Saviour Jesus Christ* (1551), Book Five (conclusion).

Our journey into the future

Over the past ten years the journey that we, as orthodox Anglicans, have taken together, has confirmed what we feared: some churches in the Anglican Communion are radically redefining the received faith, and abandoning fundamental parts of it. We recognise that many in these churches believe that the challenges they are making are Spirit-led, and necessary in order to respond to the challenges that the Church faces today.

Our own experience has been different. We have upheld the received biblical faith. We have found it to be relevant and powerful in addressing contemporary challenges. And we bear testimony to the gospel's transforming power, in our own lives and in our churches.

We have not claimed to possess the complete truth, but nor have we considered truth to be so provisional and partial, that one cannot possibly arrive at a clear judgement on theological error or unbiblical behaviour.

We recognise that the Holy Spirit of God leads God's people to truth, as they act and reflect together. We also recognise, however, that this is not just a continual process of listening and sharing, in which people are suspicious of judgements, and where there are no clear guidelines on discernment or on how to arrive at firm positions.

To deny the possibility of any access to the truth of God, suggests that God has been inadequate in making himself known to his own creation and to his creatures. It also means that final decisions, about what will count as truth in any given situation, remain with the powerful.

As those called to lead the Church, we have the responsibility not just to testify to truth, but also to uphold it and commend it. But some in the Church, in their understandable desire not to exclude anyone's voice, especially the voices of individuals and groups who are seen as vulnerable and oppressed, are now making the inclusion of all voices, opinions and testimonies into the primary means whereby we experience and commend

God's truth.

We note with deep sadness that such a view has led some churches to be prepared to include much, but be unable to recognise how they may have access to the truth of God. Therefore, having no good news about transformation of life, they have nothing to offer to the broken and disordered communities of our fallen creation.

Over the last ten years we have journeyed together in the search for a definition of faithful, orthodox Anglican identity. The Global Anglican Future Conference (GAFCON) is no new or reactive phenomenon. It is the culmination of years of witness, discussion, listening, engagement and prayer. The setting up of GAFCON came to be seen as a necessity, in order that we might meet together, affirm our identity as orthodox Anglicans, and identify the challenges to that identity, both from within the Anglican Communion and from without. We meet together as a people under biblical authority, and as a people called to mission. We meet to maintain and to strengthen the unity of the Body of Christ.

We see a parallel between contemporary events and events in England in the sixteenth century. Then, the Catholic church in England was faced with the choice of aligning itself with either Rome or Geneva. But, when forced to decide its identity, it sought to distinguish itself from both the practices of the Papacy and the excesses it associated with the more radical reformers. Now, after five centuries, a new fork in the road is appearing. Though this fork in the road may present itself publicly as a choice in relation to aberrant sexuality, the core issues are about whether or not there is one Scripture, accessible to all, and whether or not there is one Christ, accessible to all.

As we, in our time, face this dividing of the ways, we will need to depend absolutely upon God's guidance, discernment and judgement.

Jesus promised his disciples that the Holy Spirit would guide them into all truth (John 16:13). It is the Holy Spirit who provides the road map to truth, who leads God's people to the destination of truth. So we seek his guidance, in prayer together and through the word, so as to identify the direction in which he is pointing us.

Discernment is to do with seeing reality as God intends us to see it, and clarifying how God calls us to respond to it. King Solomon sought the gift of discernment, as being the most necessary gift to lead God's people (1 Kings 3:9). He asks for a disposition of heart and mind that will enable him to discern God's purpose and act for the welfare of God's people.

When St Paul addresses the divisions in the church in Corinth (1 Corinthians chapters 1-3), he identifies the heart of the problem: God's wisdom and his purpose cannot be understood by human wisdom; they can only be 'spiritually discerned', by spiritual persons taught by the Spirit (1 Corinthians 2:14-15). We come together to receive the Spirit's wisdom, a disposition of heart and mind that makes spiritual discernment possible.

We recognise in humility that we are called to share our testimonies of how God's truth judges and transforms us. We also recognise that we must uphold God's truth and act on it. Paul asks the Corinthians 'not to judge before the appointed time' (1 Corinthians 4:5), but to wait till the Lord returns. However, this is not a call for inaction and endless process. In the very next chapter, Paul does not hesitate to tell the Corinthian church that he has already passed judgement on one of their members (1 Corinthians 5:3). In prayer we seek God's judgement on his Church, and seek to act on that judgement. What might this look like in practice?

Firstly, action must be taken by leaders. The bishops of the Church are called to uphold her faith. In their relationship to the Spirit and the Holy Scriptures, they are a sign of the unity that God gives to his Church. So GAFCON is a meeting of bishops of the Church, with clergy and laity too, who seek God's way forward in our day, on the firm basis of the truth he has revealed.

Secondly, action has to be taken in public. The heroes of the faith, mentioned in the letter to the Hebrews, are celebrated for their public actions, not their feelings. Even when filled with fear, they overcame their intellectual and spiritual doubt, they discerned God's presence and will, and they acted on their faith. So GAFCON is, of necessity, a public gathering, because the issue at stake is the possibility of knowing the truth, and of obeying the truth in the public domain.

The possibility that there may be a truth that can be known

is good news for people who want to see change. Those who deny that access to the truth is possible define everything in terms of power. Their own power, of course, is challenged by the very appeal to the higher court of truth.

The fundamental question is whether the Church *is* the message, or *has* the message. Some people want to say that the Church can share experience, and worship, and work, but that it cannot share faith because expressions of faith are so personal and diverse. So, they would say, the message of the Church is that its own diversity, and its ability to live with plurality and contradiction in its own membership on matters of faith, is precisely its witness in a plural society.

But the tensions and contradictions inherent in this position have become impossible to maintain. GAFCON is saying that there are Anglicans who are unwilling for the clarity of the Bible's message to be clouded by confusion, by those who directly contradict its teaching.

Our journey is witness that the truth of God is accessible. We are convinced that God has made himself known, sufficiently for us to be able to respond to him, and make truly moral choices between obedience and disobedience. This is critically important for evangelism among the poor.

Our journey has been to challenge those who would exercise institutional power to suppress the truth. We make this challenge in the name of God's love, and in order to honour the dignity and identity of the ordinary person, who does have access to God through the Scriptures.

Our journey is to seek our identity in relation primarily to that truth.

GAFCON identifies an area of public life today which is challenged to its heart by the gospel of the Lord Jesus. GAFCON is a statement that the truth of God can be known; that it is the gateway to fulfilling and fruitful life for men and women, in marriage or celibacy, and that obedience and witness to that truth cannot be confined to the space or the form that is offered by the powerful.

GAFCON is seeking to give public and institutional

expression to the truth of the gospel in the public ordering of the Church. Far from accepting unlimited diversity and disobedience to the truth, this will mean respecting the order that God has given for authority in his Church and wholesomeness in society.

Bishops have responded to God's call to action by holding a public gathering at GAFCON. As they gather, they will look again to God's call for future action in faithful leadership of their Anglican churches.

Glossary

AABC African Anglican Bishops Conference held in October 2004 in Lagos, Nigeria. www.aabc-ng.org

ACC The Anglican Consultative Council (ACC), established in 1968, facilitates the co-operative work of the churches of the Anglican Communion, exchanges information between the provinces and churches, and helps to co-ordinate common action. It advises on the organization and structures of the Communion, and seeks to develop common policies with respect to the world mission of the church, including ecumenical matters. The ACC membership includes from one to three persons from each province. www.anglicancommunion.org

ACNA The Anglican Church in North America was inaugurated in June 2009 in Bedford, Texas. It unites (at the time of going to press) some 100,000 orthodox Anglicans in 700 parishes in 28 dioceses, in the United States of America and Canada, into a single church. It was formed in response to the request of the Global Anglican Future Conference (held in Jerusalem in June 2008), and has been formally recognised by the GAFCON Primates and welcomed by several other provinces and dioceses in the Anglican Communion.

ACoC Anglican Church of Canada. www.anglican.ca

adiaphora A Greek word meaning 'things that are indifferent'; in Anglican tradition, usually used with reference to ceremonies and robes, rather than issues concerning doctrine or morality.

Advocacy Groups A number of advocacy groups promote same-sex causes in the Anglican Communion: in the USA *Integrity,* in the UK and Nigeria *Changing Attitude* and *Lesbian and Gay Christian Movement.* Organizations and networks advocating faithfulness to biblical teaching in this field are *Exodus* (www.exodus.to), *Living Waters* (www.living-waters-uk.org), *Redeemed Lives* (www.redeemedlives.org), *NARTH* (www.narth.com), *P.A.T.H* (www.pathinfo.org) and *People can change* (www.peoplecanchange.com).

Alternative Episcopal Oversight Arrangements whereby the oversight of a congregation is entrusted to a bishop who upholds the teaching of the Bible, as traditionally understood by the churches of the Anglican Communion, this being a substitute for the geographical jurisdiction of the diocesan bishop, whose teaching or practice is contrary to the same.

AMiA Anglican Mission in the Americas, whose bishops sit in the House of Bishops of the Church of Uganda. www.theamia.org

Anglican Communion The Anglican Communion is the worldwide family of self-governing Anglican churches, or provinces, of which there are 38. They are linked by affection and common loyalty. Anglican dioceses are found in 164 countries. It has 55 million church-going members, mostly in the Global South. The President is the Archbishop of Canterbury. The Anglican Communion Office, in London, organizes the Lambeth Conference and also the meetings of the Primates.

Book of Common Prayer Also known as the Prayer Book. Composed by Archbishop Thomas Cranmer and first published in 1552, the 1662 version is accepted as a faithful expression of the teaching of Scripture, and is regarded as one of the three formularies of the Church of England. It is currently used widely throughout the Anglican Communion.

CANA The Convocation of Anglicans in North America, an initiative of the Church of Nigeria which is under the oversight of bishops of the Church of Nigeria, and whose bishops sit in the House of Bishops of the Church of Nigeria. www.canaconvocation.org

CAPA The Council of the Anglican Provinces of Africa. CAPA has provided a forum for African Anglicans to meet and discuss common concerns.

Common Cause Partnership The precursor to the ACNA (see above), the Common Cause Partnership was founded in 2005 by eight Anglican organizations, to strengthen the united and faithful witness of Anglicans in North America.

Dar es Salaam Communiqué The official statement of the Primates' Meeting in February 2007. In particular it called for the cessation of lawsuits. www.anglicancommunion.org/communion/primates/history/2007/index.cfm

ECUSA The Episcopal Church in the United States of America, now known as The Episcopal Church (TEC). www.ecusa.org

FCA The Fellowship of Confessing Anglicans began at the Global Anglican Future Conference held in Jerusalem in June 2008. It was set up by the GAFCON Primates' Council, and its nature is described in the *Statement on the Global Anglican Future* (see page 5). It is a global fellowship, with branches forming in different countries. FCA (UK and Ireland) was launched in London in July 2009, and FCA (South Africa) was launched in Port Elizabeth in September 2009.

GAFCON The Global Anglican Future Conference and Pilgrimage was held in Jerusalem in June 2008. Well over a thousand senior leaders, including 291 bishops, from 27 provinces in the Anglican Communion, came together at the invitation of seven Global South Primates, in order to pray and take counsel together. Their Chairman was the Primate of Nigeria, Archbishop Peter Akinola. The aim was to wait on God for guidance as to the future for biblically-faithful Anglicans, and also to build a network of cooperation for global mission. The event has given impetus to the GAFCON movement.

The *Statement on the Global Anglican Future* (see page 2) was composed from the contributions of many groups, large and small, meeting in the conference, and was produced at the end of the gathering. The *Statement* incorporates The Jerusalem Declaration.

GAFCON Primates' Council The Primates of Kenya, Nigeria, Rwanda, Southern Cone, Sudan, Tanzania, Uganda and West Africa called the Global Anglican Future Conference (Jerusalem, 2008), and were signatories to the *Statement on the Global Anglican Future*. As a Council they have set up the Fellowship of Confessing Anglicans. Their role is 'to authenticate   and   recognise   confessing   Anglican jurisdictions, clergy and congregations and to encourage all Anglicans to promote the gospel and defend the faith.' (see page 8).

General Convention The Triennial Meeting of the Governing Body of The Episcopal Church (ECUSA/TEC).

Global South, The The church of the Global South comprises 20 Anglican provinces, in Africa, South and South East Asia, the West Indies and South America, and represents approximately two-thirds of the Anglican Communion. The Third Global South-to-South Encounter was held by the Red Sea in 2005.

Great Commission, The The command given by the risen Lord Jesus Christ to his disciples, that they should 'go and make disciples of all nations ...' (see Matthew 28:18-20).

Jerusalem Declaration, The Produced during GAFCON in June 2008, and incorporated in the *Statement on the Global Anglican Future*, The Jerusalem Declaration sets out 14 tenets of orthodox Anglican belief. Its purpose is to define Anglican identity for contemporary Anglicans, in a way which is faithful to Scripture and to the Anglican formularies.

Kigali Statement, The This was adopted by the meeting of the Global South Primates in Rwanda, September 2006. It stated, 'We are convinced that the time has now come to take initial steps towards the formation of what will be recognised as a separate ecclesiastical structure of the Anglican Communion in the USA.' www.globalsouthanglican.org/index.php/comments/kigali_communique

Lambeth Commission on Communion, The Set up in October 2003 by Dr Rowan Williams, the Archbishop of Canterbury, at the request of the Anglican Primates, the Lambeth Commission was asked to 'include urgent and deep theological and legal reflection on the way in which the dangers [concerning developments in the Episcopal Church (USA) and the Diocese of New Westminster, Canada] we have identified at this meeting will have to be addressed.' The Commission was chaired by Archbishop Robin Eames and its report, *The Windsor Report*, was published a year later in 2004.

Lambeth Conference The conference of all Anglican bishops held every ten years at the sole invitation of the Archbishop of Canterbury. Originally held at Lambeth Palace but now at the University of Kent at Canterbury. www.lambethconference.org

Lambeth Quadrilateral The following resolution was adopted by the Lambeth Conference of 1888:

The following Articles supply a basis on which approach may be by God's blessing made towards Home Reunion:

(a) The Holy Scriptures of the Old and New Testaments, as "containing all things necessary to salvation", and as being the rule and ultimate standard of faith.

(b) The Apostles' Creed, as the Baptismal Symbol; and the Nicene Creed, as the sufficient statement of the Christian faith.

(c) The two Sacraments ordained by Christ Himself – Baptism and the Supper of the Lord – ministered with unfailing use of Christ's words of Institution, and of the elements ordained by Him.

(d) The Historic Episcopate, locally adapted in the methods of its administration to the varying needs of the nations and peoples called of God into the Unity of His Church.

Lambeth Resolution 1.10 A resolution concerning human sexuality which was passed by an overwhelming majority of bishops at the Lambeth Conference of 1998. In this resolution the Conference rejected homosexual practice as being incompatible with Scripture, and called on all Anglicans to minister pastorally and sensitively to all, irrespective of sexual orientation, and to condemn irrational fear of homosexuals, violence within marriage ... The Resolution also stated that the Conference could not advise the legitimising or blessing of same sex unions, nor the ordaining of those involved in same gender unions.

Ordinal, The   The name given to the three forms of service, incorporated in the Book of Common Prayer, for the ordaining of deacons and priests, and the consecrating of bishops, in the Church of England.   The Prayer Book Ordinal contains statements which define the Church of England's doctrinal position, and is therefore regarded as an authoritative document, one of the three formularies of the Church of England.   Each candidate for ordination in the Church of England swears to abide by the theological statements contained in the Ordinal.

Orthodox Anglican Networks and Ecclesial Bodies   These organizations advocate the transforming power of the biblical gospel.   In the USA they include the American Anglican Council (www.americananglican.org), the Anglican Communion Network (www.acn-us.org), AMiA and CANA; in   Canada,   the   Anglican   Network   in   Canada (www.anglicannetwork.ca); in the UK, Anglican Mainstream (www.anglican-mainstream.net); globally, The Global South (www.globalsouthanglican.org)   and   Forward   in   Faith International (www.forwardinfaith.com);   in Australia, The Anglican Church League (http://acl.asn.au), and in South Africa, Anglican Mainstream Southern Africa (www.anglican-mainstream.org.za).

Panel of Reference   Set up in 2005 by the Archbishop of Canterbury, this was given the mandate of considering situations where congregations were in serious dispute with their bishop, and unwilling to accept that bishop's episcopal ministry.   The Panel was only to consider cases that had been referred to it by the Archbishop of Canterbury.   It ceased its work in April 2008, having considered three of the five references it had received.

Primates   Each of the 38 provinces of the Anglican Communion has one Primate who is an Archbishop or Presiding Bishop.

Primates' Meeting   The meeting of the Primates established in 1978, and one of the four instruments of unity.   Given enhanced responsibility by the 1998 Lambeth Conference, its status has recently been called into question. www.anglicancommunion.org/communion/primates

Province There are 38 provinces in the global Anglican Communion, each having a Primate who is an Archbishop or Presiding Bishop.

Road to Lambeth, The (2006) This document was prepared at Mukono, Uganda and commended for study by the Council of the Anglican Provinces of Africa. It stated, 'We will definitely not attend any Lambeth Conference to which the violators of the Lambeth Resolution are also invited as participants or observers.'
www.globalsouthanglican.org/index.php/comments/
the_road_to_lambeth_presented_at_capa

TEC The new name for ECUSA (see above), adopted in 2006, in light of the fact that it had jurisdictions in 17 countries including Europe. www.ecusa.org

Thirty-nine Articles, The The main doctrinal statement of the Church of England, stating its position on theological issues at stake in the Protestant Reformation. Recognised as authoritative because they reflect biblical teaching, the Articles constitute one of the three formularies of the Church of England.

To Mend the Net (2002) This was 'A Proposal for the Exercise of Enhanced Responsibility by the Primates' Meeting', put forward by two Primates, Archbishop Drexel W. Gomez (West Indies) and Presiding Bishop Maurice W. Sinclair (Southern Cone).

Websites Websites run by the American Anglican Council, the Anglican Church League, the Anglican Communion Network, CANA, AMiA, Anglican Mainstream and the Global South (see **Orthodox Anglican Networks** for web-addresses), the Church of Nigeria (www.anglican-nig.org), the Diocese of Sydney (www.sydneyanglicans.net) and Anglican Mainstream New Zealand (www.anglican-mainstream.org.nz/amnz), and the blogs of Babyblue, (www.babybluecafe.blogspot.com), Titusonenine (www.kendallharmon.net/t19), An Exercise in the Fundamentals of Orthodoxy (www.peter-ould.net), Stand Firm (www.standfirminfaith.com), and Virtueonline (www.virtueonline.org), enable concerned orthodox Anglicans to keep informed and prayerful.

Windsor Report, The (2004) This was prepared by the Lambeth Commission, whose mandate spoke of the problems being experienced, as a consequence of the consecration of a practising homosexual person to the office of bishop in ECUSA, and of the need to seek a way forward which would encourage communion within the Anglican Communion. It sought to address the question of how the Anglican Communion should address relationships between its component parts in a true spirit of communion. www.anglicancommunion.org/windsor2004.

LATIMER PUBLICATIONS

Donations to support the work of the Latimer Trust can be made online via the website, www.latimertrust.org, or direct to our bank. Please contact administrator@latimertrust.org for bank details.

The Latimer Trust is Reg. Charity No. 1084337